ENDOR

"Lori is the most positive, energetic, and encouraging sales trainer I've ever worked with. She has an amazing way of making you feel like you can conquer the world and accomplish anything. She is a true professional and someone I look up to as a strong female leader in the industry. *Stealth Sales Secrets* should be your guide on how to not only navigate, but dominate, as a female in the sales world."

—Haley Ebeling
Capital Sales Representative, Stryker

"Lori's book is right in line with the way she coaches. She's a consummate professional with a sense of humor. Lori is a woman's woman who will become a lifelong friend and mentor/trainer. Regardless of where you are in your career, she will provide you with the boost you need to get to the next level in sales.

"Lori is strategic and specific in her advice and within one day of traveling with me in a new position, she was able to pinpoint both my strengths and weaknesses and provide me with a focused path toward success. She will provide you with 100 percent honesty whether you want to hear it or not, but you will find that she is spot-on in her assessments. She has continued to coach me for the past three years and most recently provided me with solid advice regarding how to negotiate a deal that had gone stale. Lori is passionate about her role as a sales coach, and it shows in the results of the people she trains."

—Sarah Rotondo
Sales Representative, Surgical Division Zimmer Biomet

"I've known Lori for over fifteen years and have watched her professionally coach and motivate our company's salespeople to surpass their goals. Using humor and a firm guiding hand, she steers salespeople to success. I've seen her help both the individual and our organization soar to higher productivity and increased earnings. Lori gets results."

—Greg Roche
Global President, Robotics and Technology Zimmer Biomet

"A powerful 'must read' book for women, by a woman who broke through the male-dominated industry of sales. If you want to know the truth and live your truth while selling with integrity and earning a six-figure-plus income, then this book is for you. With humor, stories and straightforward strategies, you'll be guided through the rough and given the secrets to succeed in sales.

"Lori MacGregor Cornetta is a sales guru who shares the power of selling with credibility and honor. The fact is, we're all selling all the time in our careers, at home with our partners, kids, friends, family and co-workers, so it's time to do it with confidence. This long-overdue book provides the stealthy, healthy way to sell and live well. Bravo!"

—Jacquelyn Jones
Jacquelyn Jones Consulting; Lead, Grow, Thrive Leadership and Business Coach

"Good teachers bring passion and lots of energy to their work. Lori is one of those teachers. In medical device sales, a highly competitive arena, Lori instills the right mindset in salespeople. She has worked with my sales team and provided successful sales tools and the right mentality time after time. My salespeople who have worked with her have a solid foundation for taking on their territory and maximizing their time in front of our customers."

—**Mike Ferris**
Zimmer Biomet Sales Leader

"Lori's passion for selling and building relationships is unmatched. Her presence, verbiage, and strategic mind helps perfect your pitch resulting in closing! Wouldn't be the sales rep I am today without her direction."

—**Carter Hehr**
Sales Representative, Surgical Division Zimmer Biomet

STEALTH
SALES
SECRETS

STEALTH SALES SECRETS

THE SMART AND SASSY WAY
FOR WOMEN
TO EARN WHAT THEY'RE WORTH
IN A SALES CAREER

Lori MacGregor Cornetta

Stonebrook Publishing
Saint Louis, Missouri

A STONEBROOK PUBLISHING BOOK

Copyright ©2021, Lori MacGregor Cornetta

Library of Congress Control Number: 2021910442

ISBN: 978-1-7370312-3-9

eBook ISBN: 978-1-7370312-4-6

www.stonebrookpublishing.net

PRINTED IN THE UNITED STATES OF AMERICA

10 9 8 7 6 5 4 3 2 1

DEDICATION

To my beloved husband Mark, who's been my rock and best friend. You're the greatest professional I've ever known. You are my superhero.

To my daughter Claire, who has surpassed my expectations for what I could have imagined my child could be. You're the light of my life.

CONTENTS

AUTHOR'S NOTE

The stories in this book are true, but names, places, and some details have been changed to protect the innocent . . . and guilty.

While medical device sales was primarily a male-dominated industry when I started, the majority of salespeople you'll meet in this book are women. That's because I want you to see yourself in these stories and in this profession from the get-go.

PREFACE

I remember trying to figure out a great name for my sales instruction and coaching company. One day, I was swimming laps in the pool when suddenly, midway through my mile, the words "Stealth Sales" popped into my mind. I'd been thinking about how I operated during my sales career and how I'd taught so many salespeople to profitably navigate their territories. One of my key strategies was to never let the customer or the competition see me coming—always be in Stealth Mode!

Stealthy Salespeople earn a customer's business by producing results through great service and products. Additionally, the Stealth Salesperson eludes her competitors by never letting them know what hit them! Customers are pleasantly surprised by excellent reps who fly in under the radar—like a Mighty Female Stealth Ninja—and then show up to give customers the best service possible. And the competitors, who never saw her coming, lose deals from right under their noses!

As a woman in the male-dominated profession of sales, I've been in the trenches and learned what does and doesn't work. Along the way, I realized that there isn't much encouragement for women to choose a sales career. I've observed and worked with many great salespeople. I've always made an effort to learn and keep growing. My goal for this book is to pass along some of my experiences and techniques to encourage more women to choose a career in sales.

I wrote this book as a sort of "things I know now that I wish I knew then"—*then* meaning when I first began my career in sales. There are many people who believe you have to be a certain way to be a successful salesperson. That's not true. If you draw upon your innate talents, work hard, and bust your behind starting out, you can create a flexible life that works for you. It may take working through five million leads, and number five-million-and-one is the sale. This job is hard. At times, there's no rhyme or reason for success in sales, but if you can keep your head up and keep going, it will pay off—and the payoff can be huge.

Nothing particularly remarkable happened to make my career so successful. I simply wanted to be exceptional at sales. I wanted to push myself every day to do the best job for my customers and the organization I represented. If you so desire, you can do it too.

Beyond a doubt, I believe that women can tap into their natural tendencies—okay, part natural, part socialized behavior—to achieve great success in sales careers. I'd like to see more of you in this profession.

Some of you aren't happy in your career, or you're contemplating what you want to do, and sales isn't on your radar. But it should be. If you've ever considered a career in sales but aren't quite ready to make the leap, this book is for you. If you're currently in sales and feel like you're beating your head against the wall, this book is for you. Maybe you love sales, but your career has stalled for some reason, or you've taken a step back to care for kids or an aging parent—this book is for you. You'll find tips and crazy (and I like to think entertaining) stories about the experiences, situations, and decisions I made in my profitable sales career that will help you get out of the rut and back into the game.

The stories and advice in this book are meant to apply to a broad variety of industries, personalities, and career paths. When I coach salespeople, I always say, "What I'm teaching you is not the only way. There are many different ways to approach different sales scenarios, ways to organize, strategize, and implement. I'm simply providing examples about how to run your sales territory and earn a good living."

The lessons I learned through these adventures made me better in sales and life. As you read my stories, I hope you'll realize that if you have the fire in your belly to sell, you have a damn good shot at making some great money. Ultimately, you can make good and bad choices and still grow your income and succeed in sales. Once you decide a career in sales is what you want, give it everything you've got. Sales is a phenomenal career choice. There are some bumps along the way, but the payoff can be a fantastic lifestyle where you provide more for yourself and/or your family.

Once you decide a career in sales is what you want, give it everything you've got.

I believe that the more tremendous females choose a career in sales, the better the sales industry becomes. People with integrity allow sales to continue to be a noble profession. Plus, more women in this world need to make a six-figure income.

The customers and organizations I've worked with have benefited from my Stealthy Strategies. I've shared this successful mindset with everyone I've coached throughout the years. I've systematically coached new hires, reps early in their sales career, managers, business owners, financial advisors, realtors, and more. So, whether you're new to sales, in a sales rut, or thinking about starting a sales career, buckle up and get ready because I'm sharing my all-time best Stealth Sales Secrets! This book will unlock your limitless earning potential in the ever-expanding field of professional sales.

However we come by our skills, women outstrip our male counterparts in every single key area for success in sales. As a woman, you already possess what you need to be successful in sales—you just need to decide how badly you want it and how hard you're prepared to work. You have to do things every day to become a force in your industry, but with the right mentality and a never-say-die attitude, women can make some major dough.

1

THE BEGINNING

I was drawn to sales from a young age. I grew up watching my dad, who was a manufacturer's rep. Among the products he sold was an ultrasonic sewing machine—early robotics—and I remember him taking me out to the garage to show me how it worked. It was revolutionary, and his excitement was palpable. When he made a sale—he called it "getting a big order"—he would come home from the office or from being on the road and yell it to all of us right as he came through the kitchen door. I jumped up and down and was so happy for him. I had no idea how much money he made, but I loved the excitement. I also remember when my dad went through some lean times, and my mom told us we needed to tighten our belt. Those highs and lows prepared me for my sales career, especially in the early days. Watching my dad's career and realizing I had a direct effect on my income through commissions helped me see that sales was for me.

My sales career started when I was around ten or eleven years old. I'd paint, decorate, and decoupage wooden keychains and purses and go around the neighborhood to sell them. First, let me say a belated thank you to my super-kind and loving neighbors who bought purses that were cute but not the least bit practical. Think for a minute about the times you've gotten into your car and thrown your purse into the passenger seat. If you had been using one of my wooden purses, it would have been a projectile that would have taken out your window!

One summer, my best friend, Mary, and I decided to put on a horse clinic for the little girls in the neighborhood. Parents would buy a spot in the clinic for their daughter, and then my horse, Steele, acted as a model for teaching the girls about taking care of a big animal. Mary and I made brochures by gluing pictures of horses I'd cut out of magazines onto folded sheets of construction paper. Inside the brochure was a list of things we would do in the clinic, including proper brushing of my horse, combing his mane and tail, giving him a bath, cleaning his gear, and riding (a.k.a. walking around while sitting on the horse). Five or six girls signed up, and it was a huge success. Steele was especially happy because he got a lot of love and attention. I think the parents were thrilled to have their daughters doing something different without having to buy them a horse; it was a win-win scenario. This was all a pretty big production, too, considering that my mom had to drive me to the barn to get my gear and Steele, then I had to ride him a couple miles back to our neighborhood for the clinic.

In high school, when raising money for the prom, my class decided to sell one-dollar chocolate bars. In an effort to raise as much money as possible and be the top seller, I'd have my mom drop me off in a big neighborhood and pick me up a few hours later. I hauled around a big case of chocolate and sold everything I had. My less than innovative sales pitch went something like this: "Would you like to buy some chocolate? It's for the senior prom." The person would say yes or no. Money would be exchanged (or not), and I'd be on to the next house. My sales pitch was lame. I had no strategy, but was persistent and sold all the chocolate bars I had. To give you the results of the most chocolate bars sold, I won—if you don't count one of my brilliant classmates who dropped off several cases of chocolate at her sister's college dorm.

Also, during high school, I had my first formal boss in my sales career—let's call her Dee. Dee was one of the greatest bosses I have ever had. I applied for a sales job working the floor at a clothing chain at a big, beautiful mall only fifteen minutes from my house. I didn't want to be a cashier; I wanted to be where the action was. Sure, I picked up clothes off the floor, straightened the changing room, and kept everything nice on the racks, but to me, the real payoff was selling the merchandise. It was music to my ears when a shopper would answer my, "Can I help you find anything?" with a resounding, "Yes!" As long as the shopper was breathing, I was going to help. It was not a high-end retail store—think Ross or TJ Maxx—but I was proud to be there.

I was seventeen and so excited to be working for Dee. She was such an upbeat and absolutely lovely individual: super cool and super kind. One day when I came into work, she shared a corporate letter with me. It said that eighteen-year-olds were the youngest employees allowed to work in their stores.

Dee gave me a wink and said, "You're older than a lot of twenty-year-olds; I'm keeping you. But let's keep your age our little secret."

I knew right then and there that I would sell everything I could in the store to make her proud. I knew very little about sales back then, but I did know a great boss. She was sharp and good to everybody.

I distinctly remember one holiday season. I wore a fluffy, white, faux-fur coat around the store while hunting for lost, confused, overwhelmed men desperate to find a gift for their girlfriend, wife, other girlfriend, mother, or whoever. I think I sold the most coats the store had ever sold. Unfortunately, on December 26, I'm positive that another record was broken for the most coats returned.

Sales is versatile. If you aren't sure whether you have the background to go into sales, think back on your own experiences.

I bet you have more experiences similar to these than you might have thought, and I'm here to tell you that those experiences can translate into a profitable income and a great lifestyle.

An Exciting Career

If I could talk to my younger self about a sales career, I'd say, "It's going to be a wild ride! You already have everything you need to be successful: You have a great attitude even when it's hard, you love connecting with people and hearing their stories, and you work hard and want to give it your best every single day. Plus, you can handle the school of hard knocks. You're going to be a six-figure earner. Trust yourself, and let 'er rip!"

I'd tell myself to always take the opportunity to learn and gain experience through observing other salespeople. Some will be amazing. They will have integrity, sharp intellect, impeccable product knowledge, and they will treat the customer and employer with respect. Others will be sloppy in their approach to the customer (or employer) and may not care, or maybe, they just don't get it. You'll learn from both.

I'd tell myself that certain upward moves in my career could take a long time but to hang in there and it will happen. In your sales career, there will be times when you'll struggle to get up in the morning, but keep doing what you're doing, and it will pay off. During these struggles, you will have an opportunity to learn and to grow, so seize the opportunity and read some good books on negotiating, sales, being successful in business, and how to enjoy the fruits of your labor—anything that will build you up and keep you moving in the right direction.

Always develop yourself, especially during tough times. Maybe you could ask your manager if you could work with the most successful rep on the team so you can learn from them and grow. It could help refresh your batteries. Maybe you could ask to work with someone in another department to understand more about your company. Think outside the box about things you can do to grow, especially when you feel stuck. You'll be amazed at the difference in your perspective.

Furthermore, you may be able to figure out what is and isn't working in your sales techniques. Try to systematically write out your strategic plans and then check off your list of accomplishments. Talk with other successful salespeople to keep your optimistic attitude. Everybody goes through tough spots at one time or another. Stay positive and get that engine revved. Things will come back around as you do your best every day and grow through the tricky times.

There are going to be amazing successes. Some successes will be acknowledged in a big way. Most will be small, everyday accomplishments. Learn how to keep those positive experiences in your head and don't allow negative, unproductive thoughts to invade your brain.

Unfortunately, there will also be people in your career who are bad news. They'll want to pull you down in the weeds. They'll take credit for your work, they'll be threatened by you, and they won't treat you well. I remember what my dad used to say: "When you stick your head above the crowd, somebody's going to try to knock it off." Unfortunately, my dad was right. Brush it off. It's not about you; it's about them.

Finally, I'd tell myself that even though it's incredibly brutal to be treated horribly by a coworker or one of your accounts, if you rise above it and stay professional, you'll gain strength and resilience. And the next time you run into a toxic personality, it will not have as much power over you.

2

A NOBLE PROFESSION

Sales makes the world go round. An organization could have the greatest product in the world, but what if they don't have anyone to put it in front of their clients or customers? What then? Salespeople keep customers happy through great service and getting feedback for improvements on a product. The right kind of salespeople—those with integrity—bring a ton of value to the customers and companies they work for.

Being the right kind of salesperson has nothing to do with being a "shark" and everything to do with approaching sales with integrity; it's about being conscientious and reliable. I once coached someone who had formerly been in marketing and moved into sales. She was having a tricky time. Even though she wanted to be in sales and was given a territory, she said she couldn't be a pushy person and didn't want to lie to people. I told her that was good, as those were not characteristics of great salespeople. I was sad to hear that was her impression of salespeople and explained that if she were pushy or lied, she'd never last or be respected. We talked extensively about how to be an exceptional salesperson, finding her unique style, and doing a great job and being forthright with her customers. She ended up doing an extraordinary job in her territory.

On the opposite end of the spectrum, I was once asked to train a new account executive for a radio station. He turned out to be a complete scumbag. Skip the Sleazebag became well known for trying to steal current clients away from other salespeople. When the account executives were out on the street selling, he was grabbing their phone calls and putting in orders with his name on them.

Before I knew much about Skip, we went on one particular call that was supposed to teach him about positioning the station and closing the deal. I'd worked incredibly hard to get in front of a particular general sales manager (GSM) at a car dealership. I had my proposal ready to go, and I was armed, dangerous, and ready to close.

Before we walked into the meeting, I told Skip not to say anything. I had a particular strategy that I was using, and he was only there to observe.

When I presented the promotion to the car dealership general manager, I held back certain information because I wanted to use it when I went in for the close. Our management told us something in our sales meeting that morning that would entice the advertisers to buy. The advertisers would receive a certain number of no-charge spots along with the paid advertising schedule that went with the promotion. The station-wide promotion was designed to get listeners to visit participating locations and register to win a trip for two to somewhere tropical. As I positioned everything (except for the bonus no-charge spots), the room was dead quiet, waiting for the customer to speak. Then Skip the Sleazebag piped up and told him my special closing offer. In disbelief, I tried to recover as best I could.

I went back later and closed the deal without the idiot coming along. Sleazy Skip did not understand strategy, and he certainly had no respect for me. That was the last time I took him on a call. If you're going on a call with someone, respect their autonomy and authority with their account and their relationship with the people involved. You should never take over and mess with their strategy or make them look bad.

Another time when I was training a new rep in my territory, I needed to wheel in my equipment for a product fair. One of my competitors had just wheeled his equipment through a doorway and let go of the door so that it smacked into me. The rep I was training was absolutely appalled. He couldn't believe what the competitor did. I told him it didn't bother me; in fact, it confirmed what I already knew: I was taking large chunks of his business. I was taking money out of his wallet, and he was throwing a "the bitch took my money" tantrum. Damn right! I was taking his money, and I wasn't done. And I never had to resort to bullshit or slam a single door in anyone's face. He didn't last long, which was unsurprising with that attitude. I might as well tell you now, I can be a bit feisty!

Credibility and integrity are absolutely vital characteristics to have in your briefcase. Be a part of the team, not a suit or a skirt; build trust. Be able to keep confidences: "Loose lips sink ships." Always be someone your customer and everyone in your company can rely on. This is not only a principled approach to the profession but also what's best for your reputation, income, and career.

One day, I ran into Ron, a senior and exceptional account executive (AE) I worked with, on a cold call at the same business. He'd gotten to the parking lot right before me. As I popped out of my car, I looked over and saw Ron. He had a big smile on his face as he leaned up against his car and lit up a smoke. As I walked over to him, he was chuckling.

Bummed out, I asked, "Are you calling on these guys?"

He told me to go on ahead and call on the business.

I asked, "Why? You got here first."

He said, "No account is worth losing a friendship over."

I thought that was tremendous. I thanked him and shot right inside, just in case he changed his mind.

As it turned out, it was a national chain, and they didn't buy any local advertising. But what I learned that day was invaluable. Ron was such a hard worker, laid back in temperament, and a class act. He was so cool about letting me call on the account. I already had a ton of respect for him, but it grew even higher that day. It taught me about taking the high road with colleagues. It will always be the right move.

Stay out of the weeds. When someone wants to pull you down, the only way they succeed is if you let them. Resist and stay true to yourself. This means doing things right all the way around. Obviously, you shouldn't snake an account from someone, put your name on a fake purchase order, or throw the company under the bus to look good for a customer, but doing things right also means working hard, doing the best you can for the customer and the company, being up front about any issues, and not selling anything you don't believe in. The majority of salespeople fall into the noble category, and for those who don't, well, people know they're slimy or cutting corners, and they'll never be respected or last. With medical devices, I'd never want to gloss over a potential issue with a product. I would think to myself, *What if it was my mother on the operating table?* Throughout my sales career, I've always been able to look in the mirror at night and know I still had my integrity.

Sales approached with integrity is what makes it a noble profession. I think people slam sales a lot because sleazebags manage to weasel their way in, just like there are a few bad apples in every profession, from managers to doctors. If you truly care about your customer, company, and the job you do, you can have a hell of a career. People can tell when you're sincere, and that's an important trust-building piece. Always prove you're the real deal by keeping confidences, whether it's about dynamics in an account, a difficult coworker, or bad news.

Integrity is not an optional side dish in a successful and rewarding sales career; it's essential to it.

Versatility and Flexibility

What I've loved, and will always love, about sales is its versatility. There are many different ways of doing things, and you can have many different outcomes. There are a multitude of ways you can approach and evaluate your sales career opportunities. When it comes down to it, no matter how you design your sales career path, if you know your product inside and out, you know your competition's strengths and weaknesses, and you're able to build bridges (relationships) everywhere you can—oh yeah, and you bust your tail every single day—you'll make a solid living.

Being a versatile salesperson will get you as far as you want to go. Things are constantly changing in the world, but all types of companies need salespeople. Once you've proven that you're results oriented, can work for all different sizes of organizations, switch industries, travel more or less, sell tangible or intangible products, do inside or outside sales—the possibilities are endless. As a versatile salesperson, you have countless options in terms of your product, organization, day-to-day work, and income. The more you put yourself out there, make some mistakes, and earn some wins, the better you'll get by learning from them.

The best way to become a versatile salesperson is to try out different things and be adaptable. Early in my days of medical device sales, my manager told me that I needed to take care of an account in a different state. It wasn't going to be my account, and I wasn't even going to be paid commission on it, but I needed to service it. The rep who was getting paid couldn't get there in time.

With my positive attitude, equipment, and little travel case of clothes, I hit the road. I'd called ahead to my outlying accounts I'd pass on the way, telling them I'd be coming by to check on them. I wanted to make sure I spent time on my accounts, too; I was going to maximize my time on the road. When I made it to the out-of-state account, I met with the staff and took care of their questions and product issues.

As I prepared to drive back home to my main territory, I decided to drive a different route. Back in the day, before the internet and all the other great tools available to salespeople, we used these old-fashioned things called maps. They were very big sheets of paper that you could fold multiple times into a nice rectangular packet. Just kidding—of course, you know what a map is! As I mapped out my road trip back home, I happened to notice a small but fairly significant town where I could prospect for business. Maybe they had a hospital I could call on and sell them some of my equipment! As it turned out, that was a great versatile move. The hospital didn't have any of my company's products. I ended up meeting with the key decision-maker and telling her about my company and its newest technology. She was very interested and told me I was welcome to bring my products down so that they could take a look at them. After scheduling our next meeting, I thanked her and headed back home.

Even though this customer was not on my account list, I convinced my boss to let me take it over. The sales rep—let's call him Absent Albert—had never pursued the account. The account was using all of our competitor's old equipment. I told my boss that letting me handle the account was worth a shot. What did he have to lose? It was going to help his bottom line more if I handled it. He was getting a big goose egg with Absent Albert, who clearly wasn't covering his territory. He asked permission to switch the account to me, and within the next few months, I converted their old equipment to my new technology. I even took a male rep from another division of ours and helped him get his equipment into the hospital.

I could have been bent out of shape because I had to service an account a long way away and wasn't going to make any money. Instead, I was flexible and went with the flow. I called on several of my accounts that were further away and was even able to pick up a new one. Understanding the importance of being a team player is great, but looking everywhere for opportunities ended up working out even more beautifully for me. Golden opportunities may come your way, just not how you expect them. If you're open and willing to be flexible and adapt, it can pay off handsomely.

Golden opportunities may come your way, just not how you expected them. If you're open and willing to be flexible and adapt, it can pay off handsomely.

Pay Structures

Companies can pay salespeople a multitude of ways, and it's helpful to have a basic understanding of how the commission system works, in addition to knowing your income needs and earning potential at each job you consider.

The pay rates in the broadcast and medical device industries were both structured with a low base plus commission and benefits. I was paid with what is called "draw against commission," in which the draw is sort of like an advance on a rep's commission salary. Here's an example of how this works: If I was paid a guaranteed base of $500 per month, I needed to sell at least enough to cover that. Anything billed over the $500 guarantee was my commission. If an AE didn't make their draw, the $500 would come out of their next month's commissions. If they didn't make their draw another month, they were probably gone, if not long gone by then.

There was a lot of incentive to hustle and increase my earning capability. I thrived on knowing I could give myself a raise by working harder and uncovering more business. There can also be many more variables in the pay structure. For example, broadcast stations paid a higher commission on direct business because they made more money than they did on agency business. That's where it got tricky for me. Sometimes, stations would start putting caps or lowering percentages paid on new business to try to keep their AEs hungry and hustling. That's when I started looking for a better opportunity.

Ultimately, pay structure in sales depends on the industry and the organization. Some salespeople are even salaried. It will always be up to you to clarify how you'll be paid. For example, if you're offered a 100 percent commission sales opportunity, no health insurance, no dental, etc., you need to think about whether you can afford to work there. If you're trying to keep a roof over your head and you have no income, taking that job is probably not the best decision.

Sales often involves extra incentives, depending on the industry. When I sold medical devices, there were many more bonus opportunities and places to earn bigger dollars. The financial bonuses were always significant, especially for quota achievers. I always worked to make my quota and win sales contests and fourth-quarter trip packages when available.

My recommendation is to look for a job with a base plus commission structure. If you haven't sold before, a job that provides sales training for their salespeople is also key. Sometimes, there are salaried entry-level positions, and once you prove yourself, you could potentially be promoted to a sales position. That's a phenomenal opportunity for someone new to sales. You get to learn the company and the products, then you have the opportunity to be promoted and increase your income.

When I was originally interviewing at radio stations in Denver during my senior year of college, those stations were not going to pay me anything or provide healthcare, training, etc., and I didn't have savings to live off while I got started. When I went to work for a big company in Charlotte, I was paid a salary. During those few months, I was able to learn about selling. Even though the salary I made was barely enough to live on, I earned experience and learned how to sell, so it paid off exponentially.

Since I was being paid so little to start, I lived with my mom and dad, paying one hundred dollars a month in rent. I think they wanted to make sure I got used to paying my own way, and it worked. I moved out the minute I found out the radio station was going to promote me to account executive.

Each time I moved to a better job, the reward outweighed the risk—a higher potential to earn more dollars. Except in the instance of moving to Denver. I made better money in Charlotte, but I wanted to live in Denver. When I contemplated moving to an entirely different part of the country, I'd already proven to myself that I could sell. I knew I could cut it in sales anywhere. At the Denver radio station, there would be bigger expenses: I'd have to pay a one-hundred-dollar monthly fee to park in a parking garage and would be overcharged for a business mobile phone. I carefully reviewed my reasons for making a change. The reward was living where I wanted to live. The risk was leaving my incredible job, great direct leadership, and amazing female colleagues. It was a wonderful place, and I didn't know if I'd ever have that kind of experience and comradery again. But I understood that sometimes you have to get uncomfortable to get where you want. Ultimately, I knew the reward outweighed the risk.

No matter how great you are, there are highs and lows with any sales pay structure. The lean times can be very humbling and make you question your effectiveness as a salesperson. One of the most important things I learned during those times is to keep a positive attitude. I also found that increasing my skill level by watching other people sell and reading books on sales helped me stay focused and get through it.

After I bought my townhouse, things got a little tricky with how much I was making and my expenses. I wore the same pair of black shoes to work for almost the whole year. I took my clothes and washed them at a laundromat because I didn't have money to buy a washer and dryer. My bank account was pretty low. Finally, I came to terms with the fact that I needed to get a roommate or sell my townhouse. I got a roommate. That was a great move. It gave me a cushion with my mortgage payment, and I was able to get a used washer and dryer and some other things fixed that I needed. It took a lot of strain off of me. I was able to get a great job, make better commissions, and eventually, my sweet roommate bought her own place.

Being flexible and figuring out what will work for you in the lean times is the best way to start out. I recommend overestimating your ability and underestimating your income. If you underestimate the amount of money you're going to make to begin with, you can better plan how to pay the bills while you're working your ass off. If you make $100,000, but you planned on making $50,000, you're going to be in a lot better shape than if you planned on making $100,000 and you make $50,000. It's better to be conservative on income when starting your sales career. Then, as you build your empire, you'll have a better sense of what kind of income you're capable of achieving.

Hindsight is always 20/20. When I was hired by a big radio station in Charlotte and made great money, I decided to buy a kickass car—a beautiful Turbo Saab. I paid way too much and ended up having a $611 monthly car payment. It was more than what I was paying for rent on my apartment. Had I bought a practical car, pocketed the remaining $400 a month, and saved it for my townhouse in Colorado, that would have been a great move. But since I was making a bigger commission, I wanted a big, fat reward, and that was the car. As you can guess, before I moved to Colorado, I sold that car and got a practical one. I negotiated the hell out of that practical car. Live and learn!

In addition to understanding income needs, one of the most important things women need to think about is giving themselves time to get on their feet with sales. It takes some time to build your empire, so it's crucial to identify what kind of cushions you might have to help you transition from the early days of sales to earning a good living. Additionally, you need to ask a lot of questions about the company that you might work for.

The Day Ain't Over Yet

While I was still a trainee during my first year in sales, I'd just completed the sales training piece of the program, and I wanted to take these newfound techniques for a spin. One technique was need-satisfying selling: Identify the need, then match what you were selling to the client's needs. I needed a target to try this out on.

The general manager at our corporate headquarters was super tough. He was at least twenty years older than me, extremely intimidating, and a well-respected leader who'd been at the company for a long time. Some mornings, we would walk into the building together, arriving at our desks at or before 7:00 a.m. Most people rolled in between 8:00 and 8:30.

When he saw me in the morning or late in the day, he would ask, "Have you sold anything yet?" I'd usually respond with some generic answer about how I was working on something.

After hearing that, he would always reply, "The day ain't over yet."

This response was highly motivating. He was saying, "Get out there and sell something—you still have time today!" I've thought of that line often in my sales career. He set the bar high, and I loved that. After hearing that response a few times, I started answering his daily query with the same line: The day ain't over yet. It always put a smile on his face.

His favorite phrase was characteristic of his high standards for himself and his staff. So, when I decided I needed a target for my new sales training techniques, my mind went straight to the tough general manager. I was putting together a company team for a big race happening in town, and I thought having him there would be great for the team and great for morale. I'd already asked him to participate, but he turned me down, saying he and his wife were going to be visiting his daughter at her college for the weekend. They wouldn't come back until late Sunday, and the race was scheduled for that Sunday morning. This meant that he would be a tough sell—a perfect self-imposed selling challenge. If I was ever going to be good in sales, I needed to apply the new selling techniques that I learned in the sales training program and get him to participate. I decided that if I could sell him on this, I could sell anybody on anything.

My plan was to get him to come back early that morning and run the race with the team. I went home, put together my strategic plan and questions using my new techniques, and set an appointment with him. I asked all the questions I knew would get him to agree: "Do you think it's important for an organization to have team players?" Of course, he did. "Do you think it's important for leadership to reach out and connect with employees?" Of course!

Through these questions, I pointed out that the team was representing our company in a race that was being hosted and sponsored by our broadcast company. As a leader, he could set a great participation example. Because of his unique position, he could promote more team spirit by showing up. Not only would he be supporting the race for which our company was a big sponsor, but he could bond with his employees on a whole different level—and get some good exercise at the same time. I sold him on the idea of coming in early, being a part of the team, and running. He came and ran the race, and it was as amazing as I'd hoped. Vindication!

Most women I know are courageous as hell, And not only that, they're never satisfied. This is a superpower in sales: you can set the bar high for yourself, and with courage and drive, you can blow yourself and everyone else away. External goals and markers of achievement will only take you so far. Take on Mount Kilimanjaro, the tough general manager, or the huge sales goal. Be willing to push yourself because you're the only person you're trying to impress.

3

FIND YOUR STARTING POINT

You may be wondering, with all the different types of sales, products, companies, industries out there in need of fantastic salespeople, how do you go about designing and navigating your sales career path? There are incredibly strategic, well-thought-out plans, and then there are fly-by-the-seat-of-your-pants plans. Always weigh risk and reward. I believe reward should always outweigh risk. As you go about searching for the opportunities you want, be creative about how you approach a sales position or an organization. Think outside the box. Try something a little different so that you can get on the hiring manager's radar, such as in the car dealership example I'll tell you about a little later.

There are multiple sales opportunities available in many different industries and organizations, depending on your education and whether you graduated from college. Higher-level sales positions with larger income potential are typically open to those who have a college degree. It's not a deal-breaker to have stopped your education before you earned a degree, but having a degree is typically required for a higher level of sales. In med device (the short name for medical device sales), a degree in anything to do with the human body is considered an advantage, but it's not a must. My degree was in communications. To me, the key is how badly you want it. If you graduated with a degree in underwater basket weaving, but you have the fire in your belly to be the best you can be in sales, then go for it. Some sales opportunities will be extremely technical, and some will not. You have to figure out what makes sense for you.

First and foremost, choosing a great company with solid products is vital. If you're working for an organization where you don't like the culture, you have some decisions to make. Can you fix it? Can you make it better by stepping up and becoming a leader? Is the company's mission not where it needs to be? How long have you been there? Have you risen above the BS and still performed well? That is key. It's one thing to hate where you work; it's another to not give it your best while you're there.

Do everything you can to be great at your job and make a strategic plan for your next steps. If you're currently in sales, you hate the company, and want to move to another company, fine. Crush it while you're there and identify where you want to go next. If you've only been there for a short time, try to get at least two years under your belt. Sometimes, things change for the better, and it's best not to look like you jump from job to job. It doesn't look good on your resume. Having a solid track record wherever you sell helps set the table for your next move.

For example, you can talk about what you have been contributing to your current sales job: "I'm the number one new business biller," or, "I've increased my territory growth by 150 percent." Whatever your positive contribution, that may be a selling point in your next career move. If you're in college and working or are in a non-sales role, do an excellent job. Always have a great attitude, so your current employer knows your effort and attitude never wavered. This can be helpful later on.

If you haven't been to college but have the fire in your belly, then go sell something. If an opportunity has been hard to find, then find somewhere you can sell whatever the product is and get a start. Once you're with a company, even if it's selling shoes at a department store, do the best you can. Always try to go the extra mile. Always show up ready to work. Have a great attitude. Make the customer feel like you're in search of the perfect shoe for them and try to build a loyal customer base—they will come back to you when they need to find the best shoes for a certain activity. Do the other things in this book to stand out positively.

Once you've built your reputation as a reliable salesperson, start to think about the next step. Maybe there's a big competitor to your current company. Maybe that store carries better quality shoes and other products, and salespeople can earn a commission, whereas there's no commission in your current role. Be versatile. Think about what you can do to keep building your career and income. Always try to get a reference letter written on your company's letterhead that you can supply to a prospective employer, or an endorsement from someone you've worked for, so you can build a story about your success. This allows you to have proof of the good work you did if your old boss leaves their job. Maybe you love retail, but you aren't being paid commissions on your sales. Maybe you love cars and have thought about selling those. Check it out. Don't limit yourself by thinking about a small arena—think and dream big. You never know what opportunities are out there until you look. Be a versatile salesperson.

Don't limit yourself by thinking about a small arena—
think and dream big.

Most job searching is done online now, but I still believe that scheduling an appointment with a hiring manager is one way to get a read on the opportunity. Here's a creative job approach you could try, for example, on a sales manager at a car dealership:

Me: Hello, Mr. Johnson. My name is Lori Cornetta. You have a tremendous organization, and I'd love to meet with you and talk about being part of your sales team.

Mr. Johnson: Thank you, Ms. Cornetta, but we don't have any openings right now.

Me: Thank you for sharing that, Mr. Johnson. I understand. I'd still like to introduce myself and sell one of your cars to you. What time works best for you?

Mr. Johnson: What? Sell one of my cars to me? (Mr. J chuckles and thinks to himself, *Ingenuity. I like that.*) I'm very busy, Ms. Cornetta.

Me: Do you drink coffee?

Mr. Johnson: Can't live without it.

Me: Me either! What does Friday look like for you? I will bring you a coffee and sell you a car.

Mr. Johnson: Thursday at 8:00 a.m. works.

Me: Excellent! What kind of coffee do you like?

See how stealthy that was? He didn't see it coming.

Now, the work begins. First, send a handwritten thank-you note to Mr. Johnson. Yes, I know. This is very old school. The handwritten note has to look clean and professional, so skip the flowers or pastel colors in favor of something modern or simple with clean lines. If you happen to have simple personalized stationery, use that. If you don't have great handwriting, use your keyboard, print it, and sign it.

Next, study the cars they sell. Go to a competitive car dealership and talk to a salesperson. Listen to what he or she features as selling points and pick up on anything you can. Definitely ask about their service and more. Try to figure out any strengths or weaknesses and learn whatever you can.

Finally, show up to your appointment early with coffee in hand. Be prepared for anything—know plenty about the product you're going to talk about. It's more about connecting with Mr. Johnson and identifying what *his* hot button is (see Chapter 14) than about a car.

Upon entering his office, look around. If you notice a photo of him and his family with skis on top of a mountain, say, "That looks like a great trip. Where were you?" Let him answer and briefly connect about his trip.

Then draw him out and find out what's important to him in a car. Ask him questions like he just walked into the showroom: Do you have a car to trade in? What did you like or not like about your current car? Will you be using it for work? How important is comfort? Does fuel efficiency matter? What color interior and exterior do you want? What's your timeline?

Give him a sample of how well you can relate to the customer and know the product line. Make sure you ask for the order: close him on the sale. If everything is going along swimmingly, say, "Let's take a look at the numbers. Are you ready to get this done today?"

At this point, it's time to come back around and see what Mr. J is thinking:

Me: Thank you for the opportunity to introduce myself to you.
Mr. Johnson: I've never had anyone try to sell my own cars to me. I like your creativity.
Me: It would be great to sell for you, Mr. Johnson. How do we make it happen?
Mr. Johnson: Well, we don't have any openings right now, but why don't you check back with me in another month.
Me: Thank you, Mr. Johnson. What can I do in the meantime to sharpen my skills or learn more?
Mr. Johnson: Here are a couple of ideas . . .
Me: Thank you again. I will follow up with you in a few weeks.

Or, Mr. Johnson could say: I'm going to have you interview with so-and-so. Let's see how that goes, and we will go from there. **Me:** That's terrific. Is there anything I should know about so-and-so before I meet with her? **Mr. J:** So-and-so likes people who know something extra about the philosophy at our dealership. She has been with our company for twenty-five-plus years. She started out in our service department. She's very passionate about excellent customer service. **Me:** Thank you very much for the help. I won't let you down.

Always use creative approaches to getting in front of decision-makers/hiring managers every chance you get. You'll be amazed at the doors that open. You may get a lot of noes, but you'll find an opportunity somewhere—be relentless.

This whole scenario could also blow up. Mr. Johnson could be a jackass and show you the door. What do you do in that case? Before you walk out the door, ask Mr. Johnson if there's another car dealership he could recommend that you talk to—another stealthy way to get what you want.

Even when you're in the door, there will be times in your sales career when you work for organizations that just don't get it. They don't get how to lead, and they don't get salespeople. I'm here to tell you: it's all good. Women are tough, and we're built to persevere even when it's hard and even when it feels like nobody understands us.

I remember thinking, *When is it going to be my turn?* Looking back, I know two things to be true. First, I had to put myself out in front of the right people and organizations and pursue those opportunities. Second, I learned a ton from every place I worked; both good and bad experiences made me the salesperson and sales coach I am today. Even though I got some pretty hard knocks and some dents along the way—I like to call that experience—they made me better every step of the way. The worst low points in my career built a tougher resilience and stronger commitment to greatness, and I became a better salesperson because it was hard on every level. Do I think every salesperson needs to be tested to be great? Absolutely not, but the ones who have been tested have a different edge than the ones who have not. I can hold my head high because even though some of the companies I worked for were not optimal, I know I gave it my best while I graced their doorstep.

Women are tough, and we're built to persevere even when it's really hard and even when it feels like nobody understands us.

From this day forward, make a pact with yourself: Give your current job everything you've got. Decide whether this is a place you want to grow, lead, or leave. Whatever you decide, make a strategic plan. Below are a few questions to get you thinking about your plans.

For the next three months:

- What can I do better?
- How's my attitude?
- What's getting in my way?
- Who do I respect at this company?
- Who gets me?
- Do they have enough power to make a difference?
- Who can I learn more from?
- Do I have an opportunity to increase my income in the way I want?

For the next six months:

- Am I making progress?
- Do I want to stay here?
- Have I been working on finding another job or making this opportunity even better?
- Do I respect my company's leaders?
- If I want to leave, have I been networking and researching other companies to potentially work for?
- What does my income tell me?

For the next nine months:

- How much progress have I made with my choices?
- What's my timeline for change?
- What do I want to achieve in the next twelve months?
- Is staying here making me better?
- What kind of earning potential do I have at this company?
- What am I doing to grow my sales techniques?
- What am I doing to increase my sales?
- Have I joined any business networking groups?
- Am I talking to people in other industries and learning about more opportunities?
- Where do I want to be financially in two years?
- Do I have at least one person in this job who gets me and how hard I work?
- Are they in a position of power to make a difference for me?

Being a hard worker is one of the most important characteristics of an exceptional salesperson. You won't make it as a high-income earner if you aren't willing to put in the work. But it's also important to work *smart*. Cutting away the fat and streamlining your most effective tools is something that comes with experience, but hopefully, the tips and tricks in this book will give you a head start in that direction.

Women know what it takes to get shit done. Doing the work is another way of saying get in there, figure out what needs to be done, and get it done. It's going to pay off.

Designating your career status updates into specific chunks of time—like three, six, and nine months—challenges you to stay focused on your goals. Personally, I wrote down my quarterly personal and professional goals every year. It didn't mean that I accomplished all of my goals, but it helped me focus on my goals and priorities for both areas of my life. For example, when I moved to Denver, I wanted to buy a townhouse and get a dog—personal goals one and two. I bought my place less than nine months after I moved here. Three months later, Harry, a nine-month-old black and white springer spaniel, became family.

I would encourage you to set aside time to figure out what you want to achieve personally and professionally for the next year. Make your goals clear and concise. Break it into quarterly chunks of time and try to keep it to the main priorities. If you write down too many things, your true goals will get lost.

When I was writing this book, I looked through old notes, articles, and paperwork I had saved over the years. I came across a banged-up white square cardboard piece of paper. It was probably from the back of a package of big white napkins. There was green permanent marker writing on one side of it. I had written my three professional goals and three personal goals for that year. It was good to see I had apparently taken those goals to heart since I still had the sheet.

Remember, it doesn't need to be fancy; it just needs to get worked.

4

BLAZE YOUR OWN TRAIL

Around the beginning of my junior year of college, I distinctly remember watching a driver of a beautiful BMW pull in front of me as I walked to my job in freezing cold weather. The snow was coming down like crazy, and I could barely feel my fingers. The driver looked cozy and warm. The driver was beautifully dressed and didn't seem to have a hair out of place. I remember thinking, *I want to make more than enough money to have a good life and drive a nice car.* I knew that I was responsible for my income. I knew it was up to me to be an earner, so I could control my income and live like I wanted to live.

You may have different reasons for wanting to be in sales or for considering sales. Money may not be the biggest driver for you; maybe you're more interested in freedom or a flexible schedule. It's important to figure out why you think a career in sales makes sense for you. That *why* will guide you in setting your career goals, deciding whether to take a new job or stay in your current job, and it will keep you going when times get tough. There are so many different reasons people choose and find success in sales: lifestyle, versatility, income. Some people love the challenge. There's no single set path in a sales career. It's full of challenges, twists, and turns, and this is one of the best parts about it—you get to blaze your own trail.

It's important to figure out why you think a career in sales makes sense for you.

I had my own reasons for choosing this career. I didn't want to be in an office all day. I knew I was extremely motivated and a self-starter, and I wanted to be able to eat and put a roof over my own head. I wanted to make great money, and I knew I'd give it everything I had to be successful. My career path has been an incredible journey and a wild ride. By the way, I also got the nice car, the handsome man, a wonderful home, a beautiful family, and a whole lot more. You can do it too!

When I was a senior at the University of Colorado, I knew I wanted to live in Denver. In the spring of that year, I interviewed with radio stations in Denver. I'd been an intern at a small radio station in Boulder. I loved the excitement around the place, and the salespeople were really cool. I knew I wanted to sell advertising, so the Denver market seemed like a great place to start. I set up meetings with the local sales managers at several of the radio stations. One of my friends, who had access to a car, kindly drove me around the city.

One terrific learning experience was with a local female sales manager. I'd had absolutely no sales training other than what I'd taught myself. Early in the interview, she sensed my lack of experience, so she took her expensive watch off and handed it to me.

"Sell me this watch," she said.

Of course, I held it and started talking about how beautiful it was—something that didn't matter. It didn't matter because it was her watch, and she already knew it was beautiful. Unless it had been a gift, she'd bought it for herself. She was well dressed and, believe me, the watch was valuable and matched her classy look. Had I asked her some questions like what was important to her about a watch, I would have uncovered why she liked it. Then I could have strategically positioned the watch as an item she probably couldn't do without. After all of that, I could have said, "What time is it?" and since I was holding her watch, I think I'd have heard the words, "You're hired!" The fact that I didn't know what to ask or say taught me a lot that day.

Instead of saying that I would work for nothing, I thanked the local sales manager for her time. I left her office thinking, *How am I going to stay afloat if I have no income? How do I try to sell and get new accounts on the radio station when I won't be able to put a roof over my head?*

As I went to station after station, it became clear that starting my career in Denver would be cost-prohibitive. All the hiring managers "loved my enthusiasm" but would only talk about straight commission sales. That meant no draw, meaning an advance on future commissions, and no benefits. It was going to take time to build my empire through that particular method.

I knew I had the drive and determination to be successful, but I hadn't saved any money from the two jobs I worked in college. Thankfully, I had no college debt—thank you, Mom and Dad! I knew I wanted to live well, and I'd always loved the stories my dad told me about sales. I had sales in my blood. I also knew I wanted sales training so that I could learn the profession the right way.

Hindsight being 20/20, I should have saved 90 percent of the money I made working in college. I did love my wardrobe back then! Too bad I hadn't planned on being able to support myself with my savings while I got a start on my sales career. Had I saved the money I made in college, I could have bought myself a few months of time to get up and running. But now I needed to be able to survive and live somewhere with a roof over my head while I built my empire.

As I kept expanding my search, I found out about a potential opportunity back in Charlotte, North Carolina, where I grew up: a big broadcast company was hiring several sales trainees. A friend of my parents knew someone in leadership at that company. I reached out, he made a phone call, and I was given an interview with the head of human resources. The HR director moved me forward in the hiring process.

The next interview was with five people in a small conference room. It was intense, but it went well, and I was invited back for the next interview.

The final interview was incredibly stressful. Seven people interviewed me in a large meeting room, and we all sat on couches arranged like a horseshoe.

They ended up hiring four people: three guys and me, all of us fresh out of college. Two of the guys were put into television sales, and the last guy and I were put into radio. The company put us through the Xerox formal sales training, exactly as I'd wanted, and I learned I'd be temporarily working at the FM station, which was located in the corporate building that also housed a mega AM radio station and the top television station in Charlotte. If I did well during and after the training, I'd become an account executive. However, I was told that the plan was to move me to Wilmington, North Carolina, which, at the time, was a very small market. Even though the Wilmington radio station was owned by the same company, I'd be out of sight and out of mind. I wanted to be visible and stay at corporate. I didn't want to be shipped off and get lost in the shuffle.

Right from the start, I knew I had to crush it in Charlotte, so I'd never be buried in some small town. I needed to stay in a bigger market to achieve the goals I wanted for myself professionally and personally. My ultimate goal was to move to back to Denver. I knew I had the determination and drive to succeed.

I remember cold calling on businesses like crazy. I called on everybody, everywhere, averaging twelve to seventeen cold calls a day. Nothing could stop me. My company and many broadcast companies had an unwritten rule for account executives: they had to be out of the office from at least 10:00 a.m. to 2:00 p.m., calling on clients or potential new businesses. I always left earlier than that and came back later. I've never been a fan of picking off the "low-hanging fruit"—I've always shaken the whole damn tree to see what falls down.

It was far more productive for me to be out on the street selling more than four hours a day. I left the office early to get on the road and came back late to follow up and do all the paperwork. I learned not to call on restaurants, especially during lunch hours, and I learned how to get in the door and get past—or win over—the gatekeeper. There were many dead ends and calls that never came to fruition, but I also came up with a lot of solid leads. I'd bring a brown bag lunch to work and eat it in the car between sales calls. I didn't waste any time. I looked for everything: a business that was new, changing its name, adding more locations, or offering some product they wanted to promote, anything that would be cause for advertising.

I remember thinking then, and throughout my sales career, that sales is really hard. There were times when I'd call on a business and see the receptionist in the nice, air-conditioned office not breaking a sweat. I'd think, *Man, I want that job!* All I'd have to do was answer the phone, book a few appointments, and stay nice and cool all day. There'd be no stress, my hair would stay nice, I wouldn't have a quota, and my income wouldn't be based on my performance. As it was, one of my biggest goals was trying not to sweat all over my potential customer's desk; I knew that would be a sales squasher.

The local sales manager—let's call her Susan—would sporadically allow me to go on sales calls with the AEs. When riding with the performers or the subpar AEs, I observed the dramatic difference between exceptional and mediocre. That has always motivated me to be exceptional.

At the end of every day, I'd meet with Susan and talk about my productive day. I was excited to tell her about potential advertisers I'd uncovered. Wanting to capitalize on me, this young lead machine, Susan started having me give the leads to the AEs. About three months before my training was going to end, I noticed the subpar AEs didn't take my solid leads seriously. So, I started giving them non-substantial leads, and they never questioned any of them. It was a waste of my time and energy since they didn't follow up on the qualified prospects.

The real, solid leads I either gave to the two productive AEs or started working them myself. Ultimately, I wanted to go on commission and work at that station and not be shipped off, but I also had to make some money for the company.

Six weeks before I was supposed to be done with my sales training program, I asked for a meeting with Susan and the general sales manager. We went into the general sales manager's office and sat down. As I'd learned, I set the table by asking some strategic questions to which I already knew the answers. Then, I proceeded to talk about how I'd love to go on commission a month and a half earlier than my training end date. I told them I could be a contributor to the bottom line beginning the following month. Talk about a stealth move! I could tell they both got a kick out of what I was saying, and they said they'd get back to me.

The following week, Susan announced that I was the new account executive. It was an amazing day. She had typed my name on a blank business card and told me my new business cards were at the printer. I was so excited. I appreciated the opportunity she gave me.

I continued to work like a maniac and eventually won an award for all the new business I cultivated. All that hard work paid off: after selling for them for a year, I was one of two people awarded the Distinguished Sales Award.

Soon, I was hired away by the number one radio station in the market. The environment there was a dream. We had a wonderful leader, and I had the privilege of working with the most talented women in the market. We had a couple of men on staff, but the women were top-shelf and killed it every single day.

One woman in particular—Blair, my mentor and amazing friend—not only helped me become a better salesperson but also saw that I'd reached the ceiling at my first job. My career had stalled, even though I was still working my tail off every day. The station had a limited audience, whereas the number one station could appeal to many different types of advertisers. Once I moved over to that station, my account list increased and so did my income. Being in a business where you're paid a commission, and you eat what you kill, you want to increase your chances of cultivating more business.

At that point, I'd stayed in Charlotte much longer than I'd planned. I had wanted to move back to Denver within three years; I ended up living in Charlotte longer. So, after four years of selling in Charlotte, learning a ton, and being incredibly productive, I started working on getting hired by a TV station in Denver. After a year of getting absolutely nowhere, my big brother—who had moved to Denver a couple of years prior— and I had a talk.

"You must not really want to move to Denver," he said.

"What do you mean?" I asked. "Of course, I do!"

"Well, if you really wanted it, you'd make it happen."

Point taken. Within two weeks, I'd booked meetings with sales managers at five Denver radio stations. I flew out and got three job offers. Within a few weeks, I had my new four-door Volkswagen Jetta packed to the roof, and I headed for Denver to sell radio—although my true desire was to sell for a particular TV station that I called C-Station.

A few years later, not in my plan, however, I fell in love with my boss. After working for Mark for quite some time and realizing he had great integrity, a superhuman work ethic, and a great sense of humor, it became clear to me he was the one. And I do mean *the one*. Although, falling in love with him created quite a dilemma. Did I want my dream job or my dream man? Because I had integrity, I couldn't continue to work with him. To me, the choice was easy. Someone like Mark only comes around once in a lifetime, and I was sold on him.

As I thought about my work options, I remembered an acquaintance back in Charlotte who sold in the medical industry. I knew he made six figures, had an expense account, and never looked like he was working very hard. That appealed to me— the six figures, I mean. A buddy of mine gave me the name of a medical device sales recruiter, and I started interviewing. The female recruiter told me I'd moved around to too many different companies, and at thirty-two, I was too old to be hired in medical device sales. I told her I'd make her look good, so just put me in front of hiring managers. She did, and I was a woman of my word. I made her look *damn* good. I was hired by a tremendous medical device company. My first year, I over-delivered on my quota by $600,000 and doubled my personal income. Not too shabby for an underrated thirty-two-year-old.

With all the twists and turns in my career, no one else could have laid out this path for me. I blazed my own trail based on what I knew about my own goals and my own strengths. As a saleswoman, there may be times when you feel like you're banging your head against the wall. You may feel like you'd rather be watching paint dry in an office and not pushing yourself hard every day. I understand. I've felt that way many times, but there's something to be said for having freedom and the ability to change your income based on how hard you work.

I blazed my own trail, constantly tried to improve my sales skills, and was as productive as possible, so my bank account would get fatter and I could live well.

Sales can certainly help support the kind of lifestyle you want. But in order to do that, it's important to consider the life you want. You're the only one who knows what you want and how determined you are, so it's absolutely vital to take some time to think about it. If you don't identify what you want, how will you know when you get there?

5

DO THE WORK

Just because other people do things a certain way, it doesn't mean that's the *only* way. Not only can you do things differently, but your unique strengths and perspective might be exactly what a company, customer, or hiring manager never knew they needed.

I've faced many challenges getting hired and selling to a reluctant advertiser or customer. Many of these challenges were because of people's preconceived perceptions of me and my capabilities. One thing I've always tried to do is lean into my strengths—especially my individuality. Rather than letting someone else put me into some restrictive notion of who they think I am or what they think I can and can't do, I say, "Watch me! Watch me prove you wrong, sucker. You don't define me—I define me."

When I was going for one of the biggest shots of my career, I knew I needed to do something different. I'd been wanting to work for a particular affiliate TV station in Denver for several years—C-Station. I'd done everything except hang off a bridge holding a sign that said *Hire me!*

Every time the hiring manager at C-Station had an objection, I addressed it. First, it was, "You haven't sold in a major market. You don't know television or this city." So, I got a job in radio sales in that city because no television station would give me a shot. Once I was there, winning contests and doing a great job at the radio station, I took the C-Station hiring manager to lunch and pitched the account executive job again. She told me I needed to sell television advertising at another TV station for a year before she would consider hiring me.

As a side note, I ran into this objection when I started out too. Companies want you to get experience, but they don't want it to be at their organization. It's a bullshit objection. I'd encourage you to challenge their thinking. Be creative—think outside the box to change their narrow train of thought. You could say something like, "I have a clean slate. I can learn the right way by working here, and I'm committed to becoming the best of the best for you," or, "I will always want you to look back and know that hiring me was one of the best decisions you made," or ask, "How did you get your start?" See if you can find a way of drawing parallels between how they got their start and adapt it to your shot at working there. You get the drift. Use your creativity and come up with something even better.

Back to my endeavors to get into television. Trying to address and annihilate her objection, I heard about a startup television station that was hiring. Hooray! They would hire me; I was sure of it! I was hungry, I'd already been working in the market, and I had advertisers I could bring over with me. After several years of trying, I was finally hired to sell television!

One year later, I'd done well at the new little television startup. I had happy advertisers and had won some sales contests. Over at C-Station, where I'd now tried to join their sales team for over three years, there was an opening. I set up an interview with the local sales manager.

After leaving the interview, I wanted to do something extra to get their attention. After all, I was going to make them a lot of money and work hard for them. While stuck in traffic, I started mulling ideas over in my head. Then BOOM! The idea came to me.

The concept was based on this: Siskel and Ebert were two famous movie critics who hosted a television show to give movies the thumbs-up or thumbs-down. I decided to reach out to a few of my current clients and ask them to write a review about the job I'd been doing for them. I was going to do a Siskel-and-Ebert-style critique with two thumbs-up to hire me. I wanted to show that hiring me would bring someone committed and creative who current advertisers liked working with. It was a simple one-sheet. I typed up each of my trusted client's comments, along with their name and company.

For example: *Lori always stays on top of our advertising schedule and communicates any changes right away. She has impeccable follow-up and is very easy to work with on any issues or problems. Sally Johnson, ABC Brake Store*

It went beautifully. I dropped it off for the hiring manager and was so excited. When I called to see where we were in the "Come on! Hire me!" process, I found out that the hiring manager had been promoted, meaning I had to interview all over again with the newly promoted local sales manager. Sometimes, you go two steps forward and then four steps back.

This new local sales manager wasn't bogged down by preconceived notions and was open to recognizing talent. Hello! Finally! Somebody who understood how to hire talented people! He wanted excellent people who could hunt. He hired me, and it was the opportunity of a lifetime. I never let him down. My first year at the television station, I won Account Executive of the Year due to all the new business I brought into the station.

Be Resourceful

Resourcefulness is useful anywhere, but it has particular advantages in sales, and the times it comes into play aren't always the most obvious. For example, when I was selling radio advertising, I always focused on seeking out opportunity. Even if it was in the seedling stage, I jumped on it. If I saw a wooden stake sticking up out of the ground, that meant something new was being built, so I was calling on that place. I found a lot of startup businesses that way. It was always important to get in on the ground floor, and many times, I was able to do just that. I knew the city well and could spot change quickly.

On this particular day, I was driving around making calls and doing my usual "radar up," looking for any opportunities. I noticed a brand-new structure being built and got very excited. It was in an area of town that had mostly restaurants and bars, so I had a good feeling it was one or the other.

I pulled into the parking lot, parked my car, and walked in to talk to one of the workmen. I asked one guy for the contact's name. He pointed to a man in a polo shirt and khaki pants and said, "You want to talk to John."

I walked over, stuck my hand out, and said, "Hi, John. I'm Lori with ABCD radio station."

John's face lit up with a smile, and he said, "Great! I've been wanting to talk with you guys." That was a rare response. In fact, for a minute, I thought I'd died and gone to heaven. I had to bring myself back down to Earth in order to talk to John.

Giddy, I replied, "That's great, John! We're here now—tell me about your place."

It turned out that John was the decision-maker, one of a group of owners who put him in charge. He started talking about the food, the entertainment, and more. Honestly, I could barely hear him over all the thoughts in my head. They went something like, *Woohoo! Another new business, and this guy loves my station! Sounds like he's going to buy a big schedule and run his ads weekly! Sounds like he'll be up and running in just a few months! I'm going to be rich!* (Okay, I just threw that last one in.)

Earth to Lori. When I tuned back in, I caught him saying, ". . . and the runway is going to go right over there."

I froze.

"I'm sorry, what?"

He repeated that the runway for the dancers was going to go right over there. All of a sudden, I became aware of the twenty-ton truck that was more than bearing down on my hopes and dreams—they were going to be crushed!

I took a deep breath and said, "John, this sounds like a great place. But I'm sorry to say, I don't think we can take advertising for a gentlemen's club. But I will check." He mentioned that he would pay cash. I knew that didn't hurt.

When I went back to the office, I knew I needed to be resourceful—and stealthy—in my approach. I needed to sell the idea to my boss in the same way that I'd found out the business was a gentlemen's club. Setting the table incorrectly would make the opportunity vaporize. Here's how the conversation went:

Boss: How's it going out there?

Me: Great! How would you like to get a new advertiser on the radio station?

Boss: Love it!

Me: This new advertiser is going to run a schedule every week, and it's probably going to be roughly $2,000 weekly in new revenue.

His mouth started to water. As I was leading him down the yellow brick road I'd created, I knew I had to get him to want to fight for this business, and by business, I meant the new money.

Me: Well, there's just one minor hiccup.

Boss: What's that?

Me: Turns out it's a gentlemen's club.

I saw the same expression cloud his face that had overtaken mine earlier that day.

Boss: I don't think we can take that advertising.

Me: The guy's willing to pay cash, and it sounds like it would be on a weekly schedule. Could you talk to Big Boss and the powers that be? Gosh, it couldn't hurt to ask—maybe we can figure something out. (Sometimes that "aw-shucks" style works on opportunistic types like this particular boss.)

That stealth approach worked, and my boss got it approved by the general sales manager. We could take the advertising dollars as long as we stayed away from using certain words in the spots.

There are many times in sales when you'll have to pull some resourcefulness out of your hat in order to make a sale happen. As a salesperson, you sell not only the customer/client, but you may also need to sell your manager or other powers that be. I believe women are the most resourceful people on the planet; look at what we make happen every day, whether it be in school, work, home, or family. Bringing this resourcefulness to your sales career is one of the best moves you can make for yourself.

As a salesperson, you sell not only the customer/client,
but you may also need to sell your manager
or other powers that be.

Anticipate

When I sold medical devices, the nurses taught me lessons every day. Some nurses shared important tidbits with me, and some let me ram my head into a wall. Either way, I learned.

The nurses I worked with in my first year set the tone for my success. One of my favorites, Nurse Natalie, taught me a powerful observation tool—to strategically anticipate.

Nurse Natalie was one of my favorites because she was ridiculously intelligent and was philanthropic with her knowledge. She taught and helped many nurses, staff, managers, and me. Nurse Natalie was the team lead for a surgical speciality, and she ran her team like a well-oiled machine. She always had exactly what the surgeon needed for a case, and sometimes even more than was needed. The doctors heavily relied on her, and so did everyone else.

One day when I'd been on the job for about a year, Nurse Natalie and I were talking about the dynamics and the flow of the operating room (OR). That was when she shared something I'd never thought of or noticed before. She told me that you could spot an exceptional nurse by watching what they do. An exceptional nurse anticipates what item or instrument the surgeon needs and has it ready before the surgeon asks for it. This might be something routine to the procedure, but it might also be something particular to that surgeon. When the nurse anticipates what the surgeon needs, the nurse is not only meticulous and reliable but also clearly knows the surgeon and knows what's next in the process. This simple action contributes to moving the surgical case along more efficiently and making the OR run effectively.

Of course, as in life, things happen in an OR that no one could possibly prepare for, but that doesn't prevent exceptional nurses from preparing for and controlling what they can. When the nurse anticipates correctly and has the next instrument in their hand, it's a subtle maneuver, and the cooperative energy in the room is stronger.

Later that day, a surgeon came to tell Nurse Natalie what she needed for a case the following day. As she rattled off the items, I realized many of them were not products the OR would normally stock. Nurse Natalie told the surgeon that she'd already gotten the items in and even a couple of different sizes of one product, just in case. The relieved look on the surgeon's face said it all. After the surgeon walked away, she said, "And that's how it's done."

An exceptional rep needs to have the same mentality of anticipation. I've always tried to think ahead regarding what the customer/account needs and then have it handled or ready before they ask. This could be anything from double-checking on something minor to showing up for something major. Being prepared and ready for anything will make you invaluable and hard to dismiss.

Anticipation is a smart tool. I prepared diligently for every proposal, making sure to think about all the different scenarios that could happen while I was presenting. Many times, I'd anticipate what my competitors were likely to lead with or leave out. I felt more confident walking in the door because I'd prepared for everything, including things that might throw me off. Confidence, knowledge, and preparedness will always stand out to customers and clients. I've seen people walk in the door and immediately make it clear that they haven't thought things through. Things can go south quickly.

Nurse Natalie anticipated what the surgeon would need for this special case and had already handled it by the time the surgeon thought to ask. That's the same message you want to relay to your customer. *I've got this!* should be ringing in your head when you first see opportunities to anticipate a need, and this will translate to how you show up in a big way. You'll subtly build trust and respect.

After you meet with a customer, take some time to reflect. What can you anticipate? What should you have done differently, or better yet, what will you do next time to be better prepared? What can you do to make everything go more smoothly next time? Did anything happen that you could have anticipated ahead of time? What appointments, meetings, or events do you have coming up where you can anticipate something needed and build your customer's confidence and trust in you? Where do you have an opportunity to show that you're more than ready?

The payoff for this short reflection is huge. You'll be more prepared and confident, which will not only translate to trust and respect from your customer but also will allow you to handle difficult situations more calmly and effectively. The more you practice strategically anticipating, the more naturally it comes.

Frequency and Reach

In one hospital where I was trying to flip the business to my company's equipment and products, everybody—doctors, staff, and administration—was on board for purchasing my equipment, except for one powerful holdout: Dr. No, who happened to be one of the top clinicians. During a meeting where all the other doctors agreed to the purchase of my medical device equipment, Dr. No convinced everyone to let him give my competitor another chance—for the umpteenth time. They had dropped the ball over and over, but Dr. No wanted to give them an opportunity to redeem themselves. He got everyone to agree to put the purchase of my equipment on hold while he called the competition. He had been using the competition's equipment—JKL Company—for years. Even though the equipment in the hospital was not especially old, the hospital was having issues with it, and there was no support from the JKL sales reps or company.

Their terrible service notwithstanding, Dr. No called the JKL reps and invited them to a meeting. During the meeting, he told them exactly what they needed to do to keep their business in the hospital. It was a huge kick in the gut to me because I'd been working so hard to convert the business. Dr. No always looked at me with disdain. Whenever I ran into him, the curt interaction would go something like this:

Dr. No: "What are you doing here again?"

Me, with a big smile on my face: "It's called service, Dr. No."

He'd walk away, shaking his head.

Even though my competitors were given an unbelievable chance to take back the business, I chose to stay in there and keep my presence up. I chose to rub some dirt on my pride and stay in the game. Several months later, after sloppy JKL reps demonstrated that they continued to be incapable, I won the deal away from them. The reps had dropped the ball again. This time, they were out. I converted all the business (except Dr. No, who took a few more years) and made sure the account was happy on every level. I took great care of them even though it had been a difficult transition.

I ended up working with Dr. No a fair amount. He became one of my favorite and most loyal doctors. We had a humorous but respectful working relationship. He always helped me keep my skills sharp and on point.

Service is as essential as getting the order. Reps who do not go to their accounts and address issues and fix problems end up hurting the company's reputation and causing a loss in revenue. Customer problems are your problems. There are many variables that are out of your control in sales, but service isn't one of them. You can *always* control how you show up for your customer. Even if your competition has an equivalent or even better product, consistently fantastic service can still set you above the competition. Great service gives you the advantage in the long term too. It will give you a great reputation and great relationships with accounts that not only increase your sales but also help you advance your broader career goals. Follow up on everything, not just a big purchase. Be consistent and reliable, anticipate their needs, and be there during the good and bad times.

Customer problems are your problems.

In my early days of selling radio, I was taught about frequency and reach. The concept was that an advertiser needed to reach their target market frequently to get those people to purchase their product. For example, if a fast-food restaurant wants to advertise a new breakfast item to females eighteen to twenty-four years old, the advertiser's goal is to run their ads frequently on a station or stations that have a lot of young eighteen- to twenty-four-year-old female listeners. The advertiser wants to reach as much of their target market as possible, as frequently as possible.

When I began coaching sales reps, I used that same theory to drive home an important point: If you're an outside sales rep, it's vital that you're visible. They need to see you frequently, and you need to go deep into your accounts. You need to stay present and on top of their business, and you need to develop connections throughout the account when possible.

Think about Dr. No's case. It took me four years to convert a single doctor to my products, but I never gave up, and it paid off. As the absent competitive reps continued to drop the ball with staff and Dr. No, I continued to shine. I was there frequently, and I reached a lot of staff members, including speaking with Dr. No every chance I got, and finally, Dr. No gave me a shot at his business. It worked beautifully. He was completely happy with the products and the service. By staying frequently/consistently visible and reaching/building relationships throughout your accounts, you're able to keep a handle on what is going on, and you stay in front of your clients/customers.

6

LEARN AND CELEBRATE

I remember my first real professional sale. I can still smell the flowers—not because of the victory; it was a charming little flower shop.

Early in my radio sales career, I earned the position of account executive and was calling on anything that moved. The flower shop's owner was the kind of woman you would want to buy flowers from. She cared deeply about the freshness of her flowers and how she designed her arrangements. She was a lovely gal, and I truly wanted to help her get more business.

The owner and I worked hard on the copy and the advertising schedule for her radio campaign, and I made sure to put everything she wanted into the advertisement. When I left her shop, I got a bit emotional because this was my first sale. I don't remember many firsts in my life, but that one I'll never forget.

Unfortunately, because I was new and still green, her little radio schedule did not produce much of an impact. My station was okay, but it would have been a better fit if she had had several locations and if I'd focused a specific promotion to get people in the door. I still stopped in to see her from time to time, and if I ever needed flowers, I went to her shop.

Learning about how radio advertising worked and didn't work was important in my career. As I became a more seasoned salesperson, I came to understand that not every business could benefit from every product I sold. I learned the importance of figuring out what business I was talking to and what my product or products could deliver, and whether a prospective business could benefit from the product or products I was selling.

When I sold to that flower shop, I didn't know my product perfectly yet, but I believed in it, and I felt strongly about helping that lovely woman increase her business. Believing in your product is absolutely vital. When you know you're offering a business a product that could be a solution to a problem or enhance their success, it makes you feel like you're helping that business. I've sold incredible intangible and tangible products; I've sold a few dogs too. When you realize your product makes a difference, you are proud and want to talk about it, and this makes you better at selling it. When the product is not made well or doesn't perform well, it's much harder to sell.

As a salesperson, your integrity is wrapped in what you're selling. When you think about selling for different companies, do your due diligence on the products. Are they well made? Is it a quality product? Would you be proud to represent the company and sell its products? If at all possible, try to talk to salespeople who work there, competing salespeople, or customers who buy the products. Try to get a solid understanding of the quality, reliability, and customer service before you go to work there. Do your best to identify exactly how the prospective customer/client will benefit from what you'll sell.

As a salesperson, your integrity is wrapped in what you're selling.

At one point in my career, I was selling a commodity product—meaning it was tangible, disposable, and other competing companies sold a similar product. Not only that, but our version wasn't as well designed as the others. Why my company, which was known for its cutting-edge technology, would choose to highlight a small, poorly designed commodity product like this was beyond me. But who was I to question? Like a good, hardworking sales rep, I showed it to my customers. I even had a customer try it. There's no other way to say this: it was crap. After my customers told me it was crap and why, I put it in the bottom of my bag and didn't try to sell it again. I wasn't going to ruin my reputation over it. I still met all my sales goals, and two years later, the product was removed from the company's product line.

You may be asking, "Why is she telling a story about her first sale and selling a product that's crap?" To be a salesperson who's extremely successful and has integrity, you must believe in your product(s). Quality product, rep reliability, and customer service are major components of doing the best job you can for your customer, yourself, and your company. Believing in the product(s) you're selling contributes to your satisfaction and sales success. It's the key element to working in this noble profession.

Never Miss an Opportunity to Shine (a.k.a. Hustle)

Early on, I worked with many talented people at a top broadcasting company. The sales team had all been given assignments to research the competition: other television and radio stations. We needed to uncover information on said competition—programming changes, on-air talent changes, new AEs, format changes, anything that would increase our knowledge of what the competition was doing. We were told to bring all the information to the next sales meeting two days later.

I had no excuse. I simply didn't put in the work for this exercise.

In broadcast sales, an account executive's role is to build and maintain advertising business for the station they represent. This means cultivating relationships with existing clients—often advertising agencies that represent multiple businesses—and finding new clients. The way I saw it, the exercise was best suited for account executives who called on advertising agencies that discussed this kind of thing all day long. Ad agencies would surely be the best source of this kind of information, as the AEs at any given station would share information such as programming changes with the advertising agencies, both to build relationships and stay on top of any ad campaigns. Therefore, ad agencies want to have their finger on the pulse of the stations in the market, so their purchases will work best for their clients' businesses.

I didn't think the exercise applied to me since 98 percent of the new business I developed was direct, not represented by advertising agencies. In fact, I only had a couple of small ad agencies. Since I was working so hard on developing new business, I didn't have my ear to the ground like some of the AEs who were in the office on the phone with their big ad agencies. In my mind, those AEs were not on the street every day, pulling new business out of thin air like I was. Plus, I wasn't close with the two small ad agencies I did cover, so they probably wouldn't have given me much information anyway. At least, those were my excuses. How was I going to get anything worthwhile from my two buyers at two tiny agencies?

Here's where I dropped the ball. First, the size or location of my ad agencies should not have made a difference. I still should have been working on those relationships, and I still should have tried to learn what I could from them. Second, and most importantly, I made a conscious decision to neglect my assignment. I didn't even try. That was a big miss. It was ridiculous to assume that these agencies wouldn't know what was going on. Why didn't I at least call and inquire? I could have even checked with my colleagues who had big agencies. They probably would have shared what they were hearing.

As you can probably guess, the morning sales meeting did not go well for me. As I listened to the other AEs giving their reports full of detailed competitive information, I started to squirm in my seat. I could see the perfect storm brewing. All too soon, eyes were on me. I nervously presented the half-assed, lame information I'd thrown together *while in the damn meeting!* My report caused a collective sigh, followed by a look that said, "Oh boy, she's in trouble," on every single colleague's face.

Fortunately, one of my cubicle mates spoke up. Well, it was fortunate for the station but not so much for me because what he shared was bombshell competitive information that I didn't know. Immediately, I felt the air go out of the room. The other AE was a pretty pompous guy, but this time, I actually think he felt bad for me. I felt sick to my stomach, embarrassed by my inadequate performance on the assignment. The station I was supposed to research had made this hot-off-the-presses change— ramping up something new with their morning show—and we all needed this key piece of information. As we were filing out of the conference room, the general sales manager told me to come into her office. I knew that it wasn't going to be pretty.

I sat there and realized how embarrassed I was. My cheeks were red hot, and my stomach felt topsy-turvy. I knew that I'd let her, my local sales manager, my colleagues, and myself down. I knew I was better than this.

She was deeply disappointed that I hadn't done my job. She had expected more from me. She said that important opportunities would present themselves from time to time, and I missed a tremendous opportunity to shine. I apologized for letting her down and promised it wouldn't happen again. It didn't.

Afterward, it all hit home. I'd talked myself out of something I had been assigned to do. My manager didn't say, "Hey, if you have some time, would you find out competitive information on Station X? It's no big deal. Just do it if you want to do it." It was an assignment.

Since learning this hard lesson, I stepped up with big and small things. Many times, I excelled at what I was asked, or I took care of things without being asked because I didn't want to let anyone down, including myself. No matter what, I showed up with bells on. It paid off. I never had to worry if I should have done more because I always gave my best effort.

Taking pride in your work means taking pride in *all* of your work. Step up, and never miss an opportunity to shine.

Premature Celebration: The Fist Bump

I'm not a big believer in superstitions, but there's one that I absolutely, 100 percent believe: never celebrate a sale until it's a done deal. One of my favorite mentors taught me that years ago. She said to never celebrate too early, or you could lose the deal. I always talked about my deals as potential sales, even when I got the deal. Not until I had the order, or the P.O. (purchase order), would I talk about it like it was a done deal. Because of this, forecasting dollars and potential product sales with my managers, who needed that information for inventories and dollar projections, was always a tap dance. But I strongly believe that premature celebration is never a good idea.

I've worked with many talented, high-energy, and driven individuals. Sometimes, it's tricky to get the younger ones to understand not to count your chickens before they hatch. Until you've got the deal, don't talk about it, get wild about it, or tell everybody you sold it. Because, sadly, it could vaporize right before your eyes. I've seen it happen, and it's never pretty.

There was one particular individual who needed to be taught this lesson. She was a tremendous, young, talented, hardworking individual. She was a little green and a little rough around the edges. I didn't realize exactly how rough and green, though.

We went to a meeting with a very difficult customer—the type to take blood out of anyone who called on him. It didn't matter if you named your firstborn after him or gave your firstborn directly to him, he still wanted to extract your soul and deplete you, just for the sport of it. Let's call him the Grinder. The Grinder was never satisfied. He always wanted a lower price, even if your company was basically giving their products to him. The Grinder didn't care. If you're in sales, at some point, you'll cross paths with a Grinder. Buckle up.

When we showed up to our appointment, the Grinder grabbed two other people and walked us into a closet. Well, actually, it was the accountant's office, but it was dark and narrow, and everyone was standing. There wasn't even enough room to sit in a small circle on the floor holding hands. My back was to the door, the young recruit was partially in front of me, and the other three were facing us. Fortunately, before our meeting, the young recruit and I had talked about our strategy. Even though she was walking in fully prepared, and she'd gotten some aggressive pricing and extra benefits approved for this account, I told her to go slowly and not give up anything until she identified what exactly the Grinder was interested in. Even though our company was prepared to negotiate generously for his business, I told her to let the Grinder work for it. Plus, we could gauge the Grinder's interest. As it turned out, that was a good move because we ended up not even sharing a quarter of what we could do—instead, we were chewed up and spit out.

As the meeting got rolling, I was aware that the Grinder was giving cues to one of the other people he'd pulled into our meeting. When the other individual, the follower, seemed to agree with my recruit, the Grinder gave a sharp, disapproving look. As the follower began to push back on the things the recruit was saying, the Grinder gave positive nonverbal feedback like a nod and a smile.

As the recruit asked some questions, she did not have the *savoir-faire* to see she was about to get eaten alive. There was a moment when the Grinder seemed to agree with her, but I felt like he was only toying with her. I was sure the Grinder was getting warmed up and ready to pounce.

In that short moment in time, the young recruit backed up so close to me I thought we were on a crowded airport shuttle. I glanced down and realized she had put her arm behind her back and was holding her fist back like she wanted a congratulatory fist pump. All I could think was, *Dude! We're not even close. What the hell are you thinking?* She thought the deal was going our way and was celebrating prematurely. She was absolutely oblivious to who she was dealing with. She thought she had ahold of the lion's tail, but unfortunately, she'd grabbed its head and didn't know it.

In that moment, the Grinder reminded me of the Cheshire Cat, and we were the mice. He had so many more things he was going to beat us up on, but the new recruit didn't even see that coming. I touched her fist bump as inconspicuously as possible. To my relief, none of the three people even noticed the sweat on my brow.

As the Grinder had done a million times before to many salespeople, he started chipping away at everything the recruit said. The recruit became dazed and confused, which was exactly what the Grinder wanted. There was definitely no agreement happening. It was all an exercise in getting the recruit to drop the prices. When the recruit answered an enticing statement that the Grinder dangled in front of her, it was swiftly slapped away. The Grinder kept at her throat by not only saying the pricing was not good enough now but also that he needed to be given prorated pricing from past years. This was when I had to stop the bleeding. We were getting nowhere.

It was apparent to me that the Grinder was not ready to buy that day. He only wanted the recruit's soul (only joking, but you get my point). The Grinder wanted to see how low we would go and what he could get for free. Fortunately, the recruit held her ground like we'd talked about.

When we shut the meeting down by saying the manager was going to need to come back with the recruit for a meeting, the Grinder and his follower left the closet. The other person he brought in, the quiet one, piped up and said she was very interested in our products. She said she would let us know the quantity they needed. We thanked her, told her we wanted her in the next meeting, and were on our way.

After that meeting, the recruit and I had a conversation about never celebrating before you get the deal—or ever during a sales call—and about being exceedingly careful not to do anything in front of the customer they could see or misinterpret that would make things go sideways. It was good that the recruit had overprepared, but she needed to start paying attention to nonverbal cues and what was actually unfolding instead of what she wanted to believe was unfolding. After our talk, she began to understand the subtle dynamics of what could go on in any meeting, and especially with multiple people. I told her about the disapproving look the Grinder gave his counterpart when she said something he didn't like. The recruit admitted she had totally missed that.

Call it a superstition, call it good sense, call it whatever you want, but prematurely celebrating a sale is never a good idea.

7

BE CONFIDENT

"Be confident" is not necessarily helpful advice. After all, in tough moments, it's not like you're trying to feel intimidated, overwhelmed, or less than confident.

Stealth reader, I hope reading about some of my experiences will help you identify your value and hold onto your inner strength. Know that through your unique experiences and background, you bring a ton to the table. Approach every situation with your unique talents tucked under your arm when you're walking in the door.

Confidence carries you through the times you need to drum up some courage and/or come across as self-assured. Walking in the door with confidence carries you to another place with whomever you're in front of. Remember that you've done everything to get to this point—to be in front of these people, get this job, sell this customer, ask for a promotion, or whatever it is you're doing. You did all the work to make it here, you know your objective, and all that's left is to show it by coming across as firm, knowledgeable, and standing on your own two feet—being confident.

*Walking in the door with confidence carries you
to another place with whomever you're in front of.
Remember that you've done everything to get to this
point—to be in front of these people, get this job,
sell this customer, ask for a promotion,
or whatever it is you're doing.*

Value Yourself

Once I was in the position of presenting my own material to a
high-level, all-male leadership team. Even the servers delivering
the coffee and tea were male. Even though I've always been
comfortable with men, it felt weird. These were high-powered,
high-octane men: all the head honchos from our sales division.

Between selling and coaching, I'd been with this organization
for over ten years. I knew everyone in the room and had even
coached some of these managers back when they were new
to sales. I'd written and designed all of my material—I was
introducing a new onboarding program I'd created—and it was
all solid.

Despite all that, I was extremely nervous, and the nervousness
showed. I flew in that same day and had to go into the meeting
cold. When I walked into the room, the energy was flat and
distant, and it kind of knocked me back. Had I been able to
chat with the guys prior to my presentation, warm up a bit,
and get a read on how their meeting had been going, I think it
would have been an easier transition. I expected more smiles,
connection, or maybe even humor. That was nowhere to be
found. Everybody was spread out in the room, so it felt like there
were many more people than there actually were, and it was hard

to make eye contact with one or two people who might have given me positive, nonverbal feedback. I was wearing a bright pink long-sleeved business top, and for some reason, I started questioning that choice in the middle of the presentation. I was holding a legal pad with my highlighted notes, even though I was well practiced in the material, and I kept looking down to find my place in the notes, then looking back up and back down again. Looking down and not being able to find what I needed exasperated me.

Even though it was all my work, my baby, I felt like I was coming across like a deer in the headlights, which was ridiculous and frustrating because it was great material, and I knew it well. As hard as I was trying to build momentum and get these guys excited about the program and models I'd developed, I didn't present my ideas in a way that made them remember the key themes on which I'd worked so hard and wanted them to grasp. I did not do what I was incredibly capable of doing. I was disappointed in myself. Then my two favorite leaders stepped in to help me grow.

After I finished presenting and most of the men left the room, the VP of sales explained that I needed to do some things differently the next time I presented. He said I'd provided too much information, which overloaded my audience and didn't give them a clear picture of the message I wanted to relay. To combat this, I should use PowerPoint, pick three important things I wanted the audience to remember, and focus on those. This was incredibly helpful, concrete feedback. He definitely gave me the gift of constructive criticism.

After the VP left the room, the president of our division spoke with me and gave me a very different kind of feedback. He said, "You're better than all of these guys. You do not need to be nervous when you present to them." The president blew my socks off. I will never forget what he said. His feedback was about how you need to look at things when you work hard, come prepared, and earn your seat at the table: all that's left is to own it. Make your mark.

There were a lot of high-powered individuals in that room for whom I had a lot of respect, but I forgot to respect myself too. Remember to respect who you are and your accomplishments before giving all the good stuff away to other people. You have "it" too. Own it and make your mark, girlfriend!

Looking the Part: The Foundation

In many sales situations, you don't want to stick out, you want to blend in. Blending in gives you the opportunity to learn a lot about your customer, your competition, and all sorts of other things. I can't tell you how many times I heard reps talk about deals and other information they probably didn't want me to have, all because they didn't realize I was a rep since most reps were male. One rep in particular ran his mouth on his cell phone in front of me because he assumed I worked there, so I got to hear about his plans for a lot of his business.

When done well, the way you dress should send the subtle, stealthy message to interviewers, colleagues, and potential or existing customers that you belong.

Always Dress Professionally

First impressions are huge, especially if you're in outside sales. Every day you need to present yourself as relatable and approachable, so you can subtly encourage current and potential customers to work with you. Before you open your mouth to speak, your prospective employer/customer/client is sizing you up. They're thinking, *Is she going to work hard for us? Is she going to take care of our business? Will she take good care of our account?* If you look like you're going to a party or a backyard picnic, does that instill trust? Does your look confuse your professional message?

When I was fresh out of college, I read *Dress for Success* by John T. Molloy. My interpretation of the book led me to hack off my hair and buy a gray skirt suit. The wool-lined suit was on sale in the summer, half off, and was beautifully made, lined and everything. Of course, it was hot as hell, but I didn't care. I had an extremely limited budget, but I knew I needed to look the part. I wanted to make sure people knew I meant business, so I wore that suit like nobody's business. When I'd have a second interview at the same company, I was fortunate enough to have my mom help me buy a couple of interchangeable items—a black skirt, a jacket, and two tops—so I could pull off several interviews at the same place. Once I was hired, I always wore a skirt, blouse, and blazer, and closed-toe practical shoes.

If you dressed successfully for the interview, that sets the tone for how you dress at work. Once you're hired, continue dressing professionally. You represent the company and yourself. Put your best foot forward walking in the door.

Do different industries have different unwritten standards of professional wear for saleswomen? Absolutely. Here's what I'd recommend: pick somewhere in the middle with your clothing choices. It's better to blend—not on the high end or low end of clothing. When done well, the way you dress should send the subtle, stealthy message to interviewers, colleagues, and potential or existing customers that you belong.

When done well, the way you dress should send the subtle, stealthy message to interviewers, colleagues, and potential or existing customers that you belong.

Balance Professional and Practical

If you're running around all day and moving lots of product, sky-high heels or open-toed shoes aren't practical.

One day after visiting a doctor's office, I was walking to my car and noticed a female sales representative loading her car, which was brimming with product samples. I happened to notice she wore Birkenstock sandals. Maybe she had a foot condition or some medical reason she was wearing those, but it did not make her look professional. It was disappointing to see. A clean pair of running shoes, flats, or loafers would be much better than a pair of casual sandals.

I used to wear nice shoes when calling on customers and would change into my running shoes when I knew I was going to be in scrubs. You need to look around and figure out what keeps you looking not only professional but also practical and appropriate.

Blend In

Look at your customer base. What clothing would help you seem more relatable? As a rep, you do not want to be showy, flashy, or over-the-top in your appearance.

I used to call on an account in the mountains. After calling on them a couple of times in my regular business attire, one of the women, bless her, pulled me aside and said, "You need to wear jeans or casual clothes when you come here. You stick out like a sore thumb, and people don't like it." I thanked her profusely and took her advice to heart. From that point on, I blended in there. It helped. I wasn't an outsider anymore.

Be Conscientious and Consistent

Find your sales style and stick with it. Are there different standards for different genders? Sure. Is it fair? No. But as my mother taught me, it's better to show up overdressed than underdressed, and if you think you're wearing too much jewelry, you are. Tone it down. Throughout my entire career, I've never worn clothing that would give someone the impression that I'm there for something other than business. Say no to too tight or too short.

When women dress like they would when going out with friends on the weekend, it sends a blurred message. As women, we're already dealing with judgment and misconception, so it's a wise move to steer clear of potential misinterpretations. Have I seen incredibly strong saleswomen dress less conservatively and be successful? Yes, but they're already established producers and have proven themselves. It's quite different for women starting out in sales or women who want to move their sales career to the next level. Think about women in leadership positions: it's better to lean toward the conservative side. You're better off being consistent and conservative with your professional clothes.

Always do your best to look the part. Clothing sets the tone and sends a message.

8

INTERVIEWING

No matter where you are in your career, interviewing can be difficult and intimidating. Many of the stories in this book can be helpful if you're looking for a new position, but in this chapter, I will share some specific tips that come directly from my coaching a particular candidate on interviews.

Morgan was interviewing with a major laser company where their sales reps were making tons of money. She was interviewing for a management role, basically to be a sales closer. She would go in after somebody had prospected and set the table, then she would close the deal.

The first interview had gone well, but the interviewer—let's call him Interview Man—was very tough. Interview Man asked Morgan what sport she loved to watch. Morgan said football. Interview Man said he loved watching soccer. Interview Man told Morgan to tell him why he should love football instead of soccer. As Morgan recounted the rest of the interview, I could tell Interview Man's plan was to frustrate her and say no to whatever she proposed. I was correct. Everything she said, Interview Man shot her ideas down. I told her the exercise was about seeing what she did when she heard "no" for an answer. The noes were designed to push Morgan to her limit and frustrate the heck out of her and to see if she would stay positive and hang in there.

In all fairness, the word "no" happens pretty regularly in sales. Being able to show it doesn't rattle you is important. Personally, I love the word no. The way I look at it—in sales only—is sometimes it means the customer needs more information.

I told Morgan that Interview Man was basically kicking the tires and metaphorically taking her out for a test drive. Sometimes, especially if the stakes are high (big income opportunities), hiring managers want to see how far they can push the candidate. This was one way of doing that.

Morgan wanted to know what I would have done in this situation. Here is what I told her: I'd first ask the interviewer a couple of questions about why he liked soccer so much. Then, I'd say, "Well, let me put it to you this way—my football players could beat up your soccer players, and that's why you should watch football." Morgan laughed. I told her that I had no idea if Interview Man would have liked that or not, but lightening things up a bit with humor could potentially help get the interviewer to laugh. Then I would have said something else to get his attention; I'd ask simple questions. In situations like these, interviewers are looking for how well or poorly you handle adverse conditions. I told her humor can sometimes diffuse a situation, but you also have to be careful because you don't want to tick somebody off. You want to lighten the mood and start winning them over. In Morgan's situation, it could show confidence and levity.

"You're smart," I told her. "Always try to read the situation. Watch the interviewer, listen to them, get a read, and decide on the fly what's going to work and go for it."

I explained that sometimes it also helps to take baby steps with questions when pitching in tricky situations. Morgan could have backed up and asked, "How many years did you play soccer?" This way, she gets the guy to open up about himself.

Maybe he never played, maybe his dad played, or maybe he's from Europe. Asking those baby-step questions could help her get an idea about how to choose her strategic approach. By stating the obvious differences between the two sports, Morgan had only widened the gap because nothing relational was happening. She should have taken baby steps with her questions to figure out what made him love soccer. Until she uncovered that answer, she would be stuck in the endless circle of "no." She needed to figure out his hot button for loving soccer, then lead him down the love-watching-football path. (See Hot Buttons, page 129.)

When Morgan made it to the next interview, she was scheduled to meet with the director of sales and another high-ranking individual in the company. She wanted my opinion about a few things she was thinking about incorporating into her interview. For one, she planned on saying, "I'm excited. I think this is a good fit." I told her saying that is like a salesperson telling the customer she's excited she's going to sell her product and she thinks her product is great. Who cares? The interviewer/customer's opinion matters here, not the interviewee/sales rep's. Instead, I suggested she say something like, "From everything you have mentioned that you need and my capabilities (or my product's capabilities), it sounds like we have a great fit."

Next, she was going to ask, "Are there any objections you have to moving forward?" I told her she could ask that, but it was inviting them to come up with an objection. It can be tricky to be that direct. I like taking a different approach: something like, "What do we need to do to make this happen?" or, "How do we make this happen?" or, "When do I start?" I suggested she start there; then, if they hemmed and hawed, she could get more direct. At that point, she would need to find out what caused them to pause: "Is there anything I can address to help you get a better picture of my commitment/abilities?"

Morgan also planned to say something like, "While working for this company, I will be honing my craft." I told her that was a dangerous thing to say and asked her why she wanted to say it. She compared it to Lebron James honing his craft as he played more basketball. While that makes sense for athletes, it has some problems in this context. First, if I heard that in an interview, I'd think the person was planning to work out the kinks in their sales techniques with my company, then once they learned, they were going to leave and sell somewhere else. Second, I'd think their sales skills were lacking. I gave Morgan a few questions to use when she felt she was getting a green light from the interviewers, meaning the interviewers sounded interested: "What's the next step?" and, "How are we going to get the ball rolling?" and, "It sounds like we are on the same page—when do I start?"

Finally, I gave her a question to use in case she felt they were dragging their feet or not being definitive about her opportunity: "Hypothetically, if blah-blah-blah wasn't an issue, would you hire me?" Let's say the hiring manager only had an entry-level position available and mentioned they couldn't afford to pay more due to the position and salary limitations. I told Morgan that if she wanted to get in the door, she might need to bite the bullet. She could negotiate by saying something like, "If I took this entry-level sales position to get in the door, would you be willing to fast-track me once a rep position becomes available?" If yes, then she might take the entry-level position.

No matter what they pull in an interview, you do not want to let on that it's frustrating or upsetting. Continue asking questions and checking in. Keep eye contact with everyone, keep a smile on your face, and use their names. Leave them wanting more. When you leave, try to thank each person by name as you shake hands and keep that eye contact going. This shows that you didn't get rattled. Keep your cool and show them what you're made of!

Be Prepared

Sometimes when you interview for a job, you may be faced with difficult, stressful situations. Be ready for anything. You need to understand that depending on the organization, the company you're interviewing with may have different priorities than another company that has interviewed you. At some companies, the management team may be looking at how you handle difficult customers. They may try to throw you off balance in the interview to see how you handle it. Being as prepared as possible, keeping your cool, and trying to connect with the person who is interviewing you will be your strongest tools.

In college, my brother told me about an open front-desk position in the residence hall where he worked as a residence advisor. I'd be helping students if they were locked out of their room, needed supplies or pool cues, dealing with too much noise, or other similar situations. Basically, the individual needed to be responsible and able to handle tricky situations. Before this, I'd tried cleaning bathrooms in an all-male dorm. Coincidentally, this only lasted a few hours before I realized my calling was *not* cleaning bathrooms. It was one of the best motivators I ever gave myself: identifying what I definitely did *not* want to do.

Prior to the formal interview, my brother introduced me to the man who would become my employer. The interview went well. He was personable and had a great sense of humor. There was a great flow to our conversation, and I provided solid references. The sticking point was that I didn't know what the job entailed. Even though I was very responsible and could do the job, I hadn't taken the time to learn the specifics.

Even though he felt I could have better represented myself by talking about specific things the job required, I got the job. I was very grateful! No more cleaning toilets. I believe because he was passionate about my growth as an individual and a female— he was one of the best feminists I'd ever met, next to my big brother—he gave me feedback on the interview. He said that even though I was funny, sharp, and had a good personality, I needed to come to the table with more substance during the interview. I should have done my homework and known more about the specifics of the job. He wanted me to pay attention and understand that I wasn't going to be able to breeze in and get hired. He was preparing me, as a sophomore, for the real world that was just around the corner. It was a great lesson.

Do your homework. You need to think about the company in a way that helps you stand out in an interview. If possible, it's always a great idea to reach out to anyone you know working within the company, as long as you know they're an ally and not an adversary.

Most people will go online and look up the company they want to work for. That's great. You definitely need to read the company's website and any articles or information you can find. But looking the company up online is a yawner. Everybody does that, and you're smarter than that. It doesn't give you anything close to the full picture, and you need to do more research than that. Use your stealth skills. Maybe you call ex-employees and talk to them about the company. Maybe you call the company and ask some questions without saying you're interviewing. You need to do your own due diligence to get a read on the organization.

Ideally, you want to talk to someone who works there, has worked there, or uses its products/services and can give you more intimate information about the company. In medical device sales, this could be a surgeon or nurse who works with the company's product. Talk to any doctors you or your family know and find out what they think of that company. Maybe your general practitioner knows a surgeon. Your GP could potentially connect you with the doctor or give you the name of someone to talk to. You may call the surgeon or nurse and find out the representation of the company is poor, but the product is wonderful.

Using all the means available to you, try to find out three great things about the company. You're looking for insight into the day-to-day operations, culture, and how the company is viewed in the market, not only for your own edification but also to show your interviewer that you're more than the average cookie-cutter, check-the-internet interested party.

Once you have the info, how do you bring it up in the interview? This is where the three great things come into play. Talk about how you've heard how happy the employees are because of the first great thing and that the second great thing has earned them a great reputation in the industry. As a backup, you'll have a third great thing in your back pocket, like you heard the company was doing so well that they're expanding or adding more sales territories.

Maybe you also uncover some things that aren't so great. Even the negative information can work in your favor. Maybe the previous rep, or the whole company, has poor customer service. No matter what you're selling, customer service is a crucial part of sales. Even with the greatest product in the world, when the shit hits the fan—and trust me, it will—the customer needs the rep and company to step up and figure out a solution.

So, in this scenario, let's say you're excellent with customer service and selling, so you take this approach: Ask the interviewer how the company does when there's a problem. Maybe the interviewer doesn't know or doesn't want to say. Since you did your homework, and you know they need your help in this area, you could talk about your track record of taking great care of customers. You could go on to talk about how this leads to more business or depending on your read of the situation, you could say that you did your homework and found that there's an opportunity to strengthen the company's position in the market by bringing someone like you on board.

If they ask how you found out so much information about the company, make sure you protect your source or be sure to clear it with the person who is giving you the intel, especially if they're a current employee. If you got your information from a customer of the company, you're probably fine.

When I was trying to get into medical device sales, I knew a man who worked for my current company who was very good friends with one of the busiest specialist surgeons around. I told him I needed him to keep my conversation confidential because I didn't want my current employer to know I was looking for another job and asked him to connect me with his surgeon friend. He connected us, and I asked the surgeon what he thought of the products that were sold by my new potential company. Interestingly, he did not use any of their equipment. When I got the job, he was one of my first targets, and I was able to convert him to my products my first year. Making this connection didn't work the way I'd originally planned, but it still had great results.

Most companies look for a positive attitude, coachability, and perseverance, but you should also ask them questions to find out what they're looking for more specifically. One of the first questions you should ask the interviewer is: How did you get your start? Maybe they started in the same job you're trying to get—relate to them on that level. Maybe your next question is: Were there any surprises, good or bad, when you took that job or this job?

It's important to understand as much as you can about the company, not only to be prepared for the interview, but for when you get the job too. The more prepared you are, the better you'll come across, both in the interview and after you start. It will also add confidence to how you feel walking in the door. And this doesn't only apply to the company where you want to work. Being prepared with an inside track as you work with a client/customer is absolutely key. You may not bring up what you know, but having that background will give you a better picture of what's going on.

It's important to understand as much as you can about the company, not only in order to be prepared for the interview, but for when you get the job too.

Connecting

Connecting is something women do best. When you talk to people with different relationships to your account or your potential company, connecting helps you get the big picture of who's who, how things work, what's changing, and other useful information. Use your connecting skills to gain perspective, be as prepared as possible, and let your light shine!

One time, I was helping a regional sales manager (RSM) find new talent. I happened to connect with this fantastic college softball player—let's call her Softball Sally—who had graduated from a good school with an exceptional athletic program. She made a good impression on the phone, and I felt positive about her potential.

Then it happened. Softball Sally sent me an email and spelled the name of our company wrong—twice! When I read the first misspelling, I thought, *Oh shoot! Sally spelled the company's name wrong!* When I read the second misspelling, my thoughts shifted to, *You have got to be kidding me!* That was too much. Softball Sally was not off to a good start and didn't represent herself well.

Despite the email debacle, I went to bat for her. We were trying to hire more women, and I liked how she came across on the phone. I wanted to give her the benefit of the doubt. I felt embarrassed that this college graduate, who came across so sharp but misspelled the name of my company twice. But I convinced the hiring manager to overlook those mistakes. Once he met her, he could get a read on her.

Fifteen minutes before he was to leave to drive an hour to meet her halfway, she canceled the interview.

Needless to say, we cut her loose. It was a swing and a miss. She was out. It wasn't the first misspelling or the second misspelling; neither of those was the end of the world, although they moved her out of first place among the candidates. The cancellation was the straw that broke the camel's back. With that, she sealed her fate to Zero Dark Zero. I couldn't and wouldn't go to bat for her after that one.

When she canceled, she made it clear that this career choice was not a priority. Maybe things had always gone her way, so she had never needed to put in much effort. Maybe her first-choice company told her they were interested. Maybe it didn't matter that much to her. Whatever the reason, it shut down her opportunity. If we had looked the other way and interviewed her at her convenience, the onus would have been on us. Had we decided to keep moving her through to the final interview, she could have blown off the director of sales, which would have made us look ridiculous.

The conversation with the hiring manager went something like this, "We need to cut her loose. She canceled last minute, is sloppy, doesn't pay attention to detail, and doesn't have her priorities straight. We can't have her on the street representing us. I'm not putting her in front of the director even if she would have been fantastic."

The conversation with Softball Sally went something like this, "As we previously discussed, your email had two misspellings of the company name. That wasn't great, but it wasn't a deal-breaker. Canceling the interview last minute was the deal-breaker. We need to go in a different direction." I felt like saying, "We need to go in the complete opposite direction you're going in," but why waste the words?

Sally's sloppy email translated to not paying attention to detail, proofreading, or doing her homework on a company she was about to contact, so why would she be any more professional representing us on a sales call? She had the opportunity to meet someone who had the power to hire her for a job that could make her six figures in two to three years. She didn't capitalize on this huge opportunity, so why would she show a better handle on her priorities in this highly self-driven job? Opportunities don't come around like that every day. There were plenty of other candidates who would understand the great opportunity and would have loved a shot like that. Canceling at the last minute showed disregard for others. Hiring managers don't want someone like that representing them to their clients/customers, nor do they want to work with someone who is inconsiderate.

Other Important Practices

When you're new to the professional world, there are a few things that may feel small but are incredibly important. Let's explore those.

In any type of written correspondence, names must be spelled correctly. Furthermore, everything in the email should be spelled correctly. Your writing needs to be sharp, concise, and to the point. If you aren't sure if something is written well or punctuated properly, do everything you can to make sure it's correct. Maybe you have a friend who's great at proofreading and editing, or maybe you have an old teacher who would be willing to help you. Either way, what you write is your responsibility. It's a reflection of you and the kind of worker you'll be. So, make sure everything you do is top-shelf. You're being evaluated the second you make contact.

In the same vein, if you aren't sure how to pronounce something, like the name of the company, call them. Listen for the receptionist or voicemail to hear the correct pronunciation. Then practice the heck out of saying it. You want the name to sound natural coming out of your mouth. Remember, you want it to come across like you're a natural fit. Pronouncing the name of the company correctly is key.

For example, about thirty years ago, "endoscopy" was not a word you heard very often, if at all. The company I wanted to sell for had that word in the name. I called the company to hear the receptionist say it properly. It was important to find that out. Once I learned the correct pronunciation, I wrote it down like it sounded. Then I said it out loud several times until pronouncing it was natural.

A few things the hiring manager may be thinking the entire time they're interacting with you are:

- Will this individual represent our company well?
- Is she going to misspell words when she sends an email to our biggest customer?
- Is she going to cancel an important meeting like it's no big deal?
- Does she pay attention to detail?
- Is she who she says she is?

Whether you're new to job hunting or a seasoned interviewer, keep an eye on the little stuff, the details, so you get the chance to move forward in the hiring process. Remember, from the minute you make contact, you're under a microscope. Make sure you have your i's dotted, t's crossed, and ducks in a row. You must be polished on every level. Don't be a Softball Sally.

Final Interview Throwdown

In the top-floor conference room at a downtown hotel, I sat in a chair directly across from the acting director of sales (DOS), who was temporarily filling in as DOS. He was from a different division, and the other individual was the newly promoted regional sales manager (RSM), who would be my boss. They were sitting on a couch with a coffee table between us, interviewing me. The room felt cavernous.

After meeting every challenge and deterrent the RSM had thrown at me, I was in the final stages of a long and involved interview process, and I was giving them the full-court press. "When do I start?" was one of the questions I had in my arsenal. I was going to kick off with that question after we covered theirs.

During the interview, the temporary DOS asked me a question that I still cannot believe. He looked me square in the eye and, with all the seriousness in the world, asked me if I wanted to be in medical sales so I could marry a surgeon.

I remember thinking, *WHAT? Did he just say that out loud?* I was flabbergasted. I've never been one of those people who has a great snappy comeback when somebody says something ludicrous, but on this particular day, all the stars aligned, and to this day, I'm proud of my response.

Even though I was in love and knew the man I wanted to marry, I thought, *I'm not going to justify that ludicrous question with an answer about my life.* I looked across the table at both of them and said, "I don't know what the future holds for me, but I will tell you this." I took a significant pause. "You don't want me"—another pause, so they could feel the gravity of my words because I knew this was true with every ounce of my body—"selling against you." After I left, they probably both had to change their pants.

The response hung over them like the cloud of doom. The interview went on, and the temporary DOS asked other stupid questions like what kind of animal I'd be if I had to choose one. I continued to think, *Are these two for real? Am I going to work with a bunch of Neanderthals?* Then I thought, *I'll kick their door down.*

Keep in mind, I was coming from an incredibly progressive broadcast company where leadership positions were based on merit. Women and men were judged on who was best for the job, not gender. Revolutionary.

After the interview, even though I felt I'd definitely given it my best, I knew I needed to do some kind of big gesture. This was a big old boys' club, and I needed to set myself apart from the likely all-male candidates I was up against. I decided a signature thank you would work. I handpicked local snacks—chocolates, peanuts, crackers, and the like—to fill a small basket and had it beautifully wrapped in clear cellophane, so you could see all the delicious snacks and my handwritten thank-you note inside. I dropped off the classy basket at the front desk of the hotel and asked them to deliver it to the acting DOS—let's call him Zippy.

A few days later, I asked the RSM—let's call him Kenny—if Zippy had gotten the basket. He said he hadn't heard anything about it, but he would ask. When he called me back, he told me Zippy thought the basket was something from the hotel and never bothered to open it. It obviously didn't make a difference, but I'm glad I did it. You may be thinking, *Why would she make that basket for that jerk?* I was looking at the bigger picture. I wanted in. I knew I could crush the job, and I wanted to be different from the guys who were no doubt interviewing. I was sure they were not going to handpick items for a basket and deliver a handwritten thank-you note.

The following week, I was hired, and it was life-changing. Fortunately, by the time I started working for the company, there was a great, new director of sales, and Zippy had returned to the comfort of his cave.

When you know what you want, sometimes, you have to figuratively kick the door down to get it. I knew this could be an incredible opportunity to grow my net worth. I wanted in, and I wasn't going to let some idiot man stop me. I doubled my income in my first year and continued to increase it annually. Plus, I loved the job. My customers and many people who worked for the company were fantastic.

I remember thinking that this job was going to be completely different from anything I'd done before, but I felt in my bones it was an opportunity of a lifetime. Those men were protecting it so ardently, not wanting to let outsiders or females in, that it confirmed it must be good, and it made me think, *Open the door up, or I'm going to f***ing kick it down!* I knew in my heart of hearts I had the grit, determination, and the relentless ability to crush anything I put my mind to. And if those two boobs had made leadership, I sure as hell could do the job. I was fierce and knew I could run circles around them, so I bet on myself.

9

FIRST IMPRESSIONS

Years ago, when my daughter was in her formative years, she attended a wonderful school. Every month, there was a big assembly for both the lower school and middle schools. At times, I felt like I was a student, especially when the head of school spoke to the students. He was truly one of the kindest, most considerate people on the planet. He was so highly respected because he lived what he taught. He was the real deal. One particular all-school assembly message will stay with me forever.

The head of school was talking about pitching in and doing considerate deeds. He mentioned picking up a piece of trash on the school campus, helping someone who was struggling, and generally thinking of others. He challenged all students—and I believe the parents—to think about making kind, considerate choices in their lives. The gymnasium was always quiet when he spoke; there were no whispers, even from the parents.

The next thing he said filled the gym with hope. He asked, "Who are you when no one is looking? It's easy to do the right thing when you know your teacher or someone is watching you, but what choices do you make when it's only you?"

This hit home with me. It made me stop and think, *Who am I when no one is looking?* I always try to bring in an abandoned shopping cart in a grocery store parking lot, especially if it looks like it could roll into a car or it's in the accessible parking area. Professionally, whenever I've had to make a decision about a questionable strategy or risky professional move, the question took this form: If I owned/ran this company, what would I want my employee to do? I often think of that head of school and hear his voice when I do those things.

I shared the "Who are you when no one is looking?" question with a particularly green sales rep. We were going to drive to some accounts that were a few hours away from the bulk of her territory, and we stopped by an account on the way out of town. As we were walking in, she mentioned a small part, a widget, that our company made. She needed one to show to one of the accounts we were going to visit. The account we were now walking into bought the widgets all the time and had plenty in stock, and she said that she was planning to take one with her.

I stopped her dead in her tracks. I asked her why she wouldn't ask the customer if it would be okay to take one. She said it was no big deal, and no one would even notice. I told her that was not the point. I asked if it belonged to her. She said no, but it was her product. I explained that if something doesn't belong to you, you have to ask. That's being respectful and appropriate and not taking anything for granted. She hadn't thought it through.

I asked her if she would walk into a friend's house and take something she thought the friend wouldn't even miss. She emphatically said, "Of course not." Then I asked, "So, what's the difference?" Did she think her friend would invite her back over if they noticed she'd taken something? Did she think her friend would tell other friends? Maybe it would end up hurting her reputation. What did she think her customer would do if they walked in while she had her hand in the widget box? Something that seems small could easily blow up in her face. That was when I shared the head of school's insightful question with her.

When we arrived in the department where the widgets were kept, she asked the customer if we could have one.

The customer said, "Absolutely! Take as many as you need."

The rep looked at her and said, "We only need one."

We left, and we all had smiles on our faces. It was no big deal for her to ask the customer; my question to her afterward was, "Why would you have risked it at all?"

Who are you when no one is looking? Remember, you're the person you're trying to impress.

Mind Your Face

Early in my career, I remember a manager asked me, "Is everything okay?" She said I didn't seem like my normal, happy self. I was frustrated that things weren't coming together exactly as I wanted them. But when she asked that question, I realized I needed to slap a smile on my face and get over it.

Have you ever seen the movie *Moonstruck*? In the movie, Nicholas Cage's character confesses his love to Cher's character. She was engaged to his brother and proceeded to slap him across the face and told him to snap out of it. Even though no one was professing their love to me, I knew I needed to snap out of it and slap a smile on my face.

Women are, unfortunately, experts at masking what's really going on. But that comes in handy in sales. When you're smiling and upbeat, no matter what, it helps to make other people feel that way. If you look solemn and are scowling, you don't look approachable, and you aren't facilitating connections or conversations with people.

I remember working with a young man who had recently finished his career as a professional football player. He wanted to be in sales, and this was his first sales job. I'd been brought in because there was a 911 situation happening with him. His sales manager told me she was contemplating firing him for several reasons. The in-house people didn't want to work with him because he was obnoxious, and the manager was worried that he didn't relate well to his customers. She wanted me to get in there, figure out what the heck was going on, determine whether the guy had the potential to succeed, and see if I could get him on track. The manager wanted to keep him, but her boss told her it wasn't working out and it was probably time to let him go. I was the rep's last chance. Of course, he didn't know anything about it.

I flew in to work with him for a few days. Let's call him Scowling Sam. Sam had a meeting and wasn't able to pick me up at the airport, but his boss, who lived in town, did. We had a brief lunch meeting where she shared some more examples of what was going wrong with the rep.

When the time came to meet Scowling Sam, his boss drove me to a wide-open dirt lot. There were no other cars around. We waited. The rep drove up in his car and parked a few yards away, facing us like he was going to ram us (albeit jokingly).

When we got out of our cars, I looked at the rep and couldn't help but think he looked like a huge bull that was about to burst from the gate at a rodeo. The scowl on his face was monumental. As I walked toward him, I tried to think of reasons why he looked so mad. Maybe he'd stubbed his toe earlier that day. Maybe he hadn't eaten all day. Maybe he was ticked that he wasn't a woman. Whatever the reason, he looked pissed.

Scowling Sam was a massive guy, so he looked cranky and terrifying all at the same time. I wasn't terrified, but I didn't feel warm and fuzzy either.

When we shook hands and his manager introduced us, he still scowled. That scowl had been successful for his position in professional football, but it was an absolute buzzkill for sales. I was sure he got the attention of whoever he was facing on the opposing team, but that wasn't going to work when he should be building connections and relationships with his accounts.

Since his negative facial expression was hurting him in front of the customer, I thought it was likely also affecting how he came across to the in-house support staff on the phone. He came off a little obnoxious and a little nasty; people can pick up on that over the phone. I knew Scowling Sam had to immediately correct those big issues. The in-house people played a huge role in a rep's success or failure to deliver to the customer. They were crucial to everything from product issues to timely order delivery.

As we worked together the rest of that day, I could hear his frustration. He was driven, competitive, and a hard worker, but things were not coming together for him. He wasn't organized, and he was doing things that were working against him. It was clear he had no idea about any of the negative things he was doing because he'd never sold before. He needed to start listening, stop chewing gum on calls, and get organized. He also needed to be a little more relaxed in front of customers to help them feel more relaxed around him. All of those things, plus he needed to quit scaring the hell out of people. Scowling Sam's job depended on it.

When we wrapped up our first day, I carefully laid everything out on the table. I talked about how he could come across as being obnoxious even though I knew he wasn't and didn't mean to be. I told him he could be rubbing people the wrong way with his attitude and a few habits. I explained that the scowl he used in football was killing him in sales; he had to stop that immediately and start smiling. I explained how the things I observed were getting in his way and stopping him from achieving all he wanted. Fortunately, he was coachable. He listened and took everything to heart.

The next day, he was a changed man. He smiled at everybody. He did a much better job listening and made an effort to be relaxed and comfortable in front of customers. He was smiling and connecting with people—Smiling Sam was a hit!

As I walked behind him through an account that day, all the people we passed had big smiles on their faces. I joked around, asking him what he was doing up there where I couldn't see his face, and he chuckled and said his cheeks were hurting because he was smiling so much. I told him to keep up the great work. People seemed far more comfortable around him. We were able to get some good information and leave behind some smiling people.

After working with him a few days, and especially after witnessing his rapid improvement and how he embraced and implemented the constructive feedback, I recommended that his manager keep him on board. She did, and Smiling Sam ended up being one of the biggest producers in her region.

Never underestimate the power of a smile. Smiling and being genuine will not only positively impact your customers but also contribute to your job satisfaction.

Smiling and being genuine will not only positively impact your customers but also contribute to your job satisfaction.

Try it. Smile at people all day long. When you have a smile on your face and you're warm with people, people will usually respond positively to you. If you haven't tried it, then you owe it to yourself to do it. It's an incredibly simple and straightforward change, and you'll be amazed at the results.

You Don't Need to Be a Comedian to Make Them Laugh

Successful saleswomen don't need to be experts at telling jokes, but they do know how to use a sense of humor to break the ice, diffuse a tense situation, and connect.

Some of the greatest salespeople I've ever known are also some of the funniest people I've ever met. The most highly successful saleswomen possess a tremendous sense of humor. I believe they're even more successful because they have a humorous way about them.

I don't have any proof of this next observation, but I believe when people are funny or know how to move things along with humor, customers perceive a higher level of confidence. There's something about a witty individual who can keep the conversation moving and earn a seat at the table.

However, humor can be finicky. You have to know your audience and know your style. I've had a few jokes bomb over the years. Once, I was coaching a rep and decided in all my wisdom to tell a joke to his customers. I don't know what possessed me to do that; I think I wanted to break the ice and lighten the mood. Typically, I did this using the Stealth Sales Starters (see Chapter 17). Usually, I'd never start with a joke. But for some reason, I thought a joke was a great idea.

Learn from me—you don't need a joke. When I told the joke to the two men, they stared at me like I was smiling with a bunch of spinach stuck between my teeth. It was not good. And then they started whispering to each other, which was really not good! That was the last time I told a joke to people I didn't know. I learned my "This is no joke" lesson and never did that again. Good humor requires knowing your audience and your style, and I was out of my depth in both pools!

Despite that particular bomb, humor has served me well over the years. This next story is about how I got myself on the map in a male-dominated sales organization. It was not planned and will go down in the record books as my shock-and-awe approach, my "Here I am, deal with it" philosophy.

I'd been selling for my company for a year. I'd crushed my sales quota and earned a prestigious award. The following night, our very funny marketing/operations team did a banquet with a "roast" type award ceremony for the sales reps. This company had an abundance of truly hilarious people. I always felt like I was with my people on the mothership when I attended these fantastic meetings. They always recharged my batteries. It was a thrill being around supercharged successful salespeople, leadership, and staff.

The night of the first—and I believe the last—time my division ever did an Operations Banquet, it was a night of spoof awards given to some select sales reps by the marketing team. As it turned out, I was the first one to receive a spoof award. It was a hilarious award based on the comments I'd made in a video interview earlier that year. In the video, I'd been asked what I loved about my job. Trying to be creative and funny at the same time, I made a comment about how I loved that "legal tender" and that was what got me going every day.

The funny marketing guy who gave my award said it was the Gordon Gecko award. This was based on Michael Douglas's character in the movie *Wall Street*, when Gordon Gecko says, "Greed is good." It was a hilarious award, and I was cracking up as I was walked up on stage. The emcee told me I needed to say something. On the fly, and with tons of adrenaline coursing through my body, I leaned into the microphone and roared, "Yippee-ki-yay, motherf*****!" Well, if you know the line from Bruce Willis's character in the first *Die Hard* movie, you know what I said. The room erupted in a roar of laughter.

After the banquet ended, guys were slapping me on the back, telling me how funny I was, hugging me, and sharing people's reactions to what I said. Apparently, one of the leaders laughed so hard, he leaned back in his chair and almost went flying backward. It was a great night. Needless to say, they appreciated my sense of humor.

This type of humor was much more my speed. Plus, I knew my audience. The *Die Hard* franchise was still putting out movies, and the audience was mostly men. They and the women in the audience were mostly young and action-packed people; I figured 99 percent of them would get it. Even if they didn't know where the line came from, it was a hilarious line.

A solid sense of humor is extremely handy in sales. Jokes are probably the toughest way to do humor well; they can be deadly and don't provide flow to a conversation or situation. But having a solid sense of humor or wittiness can. When used properly, it can be a stealth approach to unify people, neutralize tricky situations, soften the blow on something tough, or put you on the map in your organization. It can help you build relationships with other people, whether they have a similar sense of humor or not, and even strengthen relationships when used at the right time.

Having a sense of humor in sales will keep you sane.

There are many different types of humor. Sometimes, someone who rarely says anything will say something that's hilarious. Sometimes, people have a dry sense of humor. Some people are quick-witted. Some are great at quotes or voices. Start to pay attention to your own kind of humor.

If you don't feel funny, start by thinking funny things—talk to yourself and try to say funny things to crack yourself up. You could say something funny about a situation. For example, if you spill coffee on yourself, don't think or say something like "Ha-ha, I'm such a klutz." I don't like the idea of putting yourself down, and it puts the other person or people in a weird, uncomfortable spot. Instead, you could think or say, "I always wanted to design my own clothing," or, "I was chilly and thought I could warm myself up, so I dumped hot coffee on myself."

Next, take one of your clever thoughts for a ride by saying it out loud. Let's say you've been standing in a line for twenty minutes. It doesn't seem to be moving at all. You say to the person in front of you, "I'm so glad I have nothing else to do," or, "Isn't it great this line is moving along so quickly!" Sometimes by stating the exact opposite of what's happening, you can make people lighten up and laugh. Sometimes, you can throw in a funny line from a popular movie. The more you practice thinking funny things and saying something clever out loud, the more successful you'll be when you feel the need for some humor.

If you're not sure about this humor thing, start practicing on a smaller scale. Say something humorous to a colleague and see how it goes. If successful, then keep going. If not, regroup and try a different humorous approach.

You'll get the hang of it. Then, when you need a little levity in a business setting, you'll have the confidence to use your sense of humor.

10

GET ORGANIZED

Organization is as important as attitude, listening, product knowledge, and being a self-starter. It's an essential ingredient for your success, as it affects professionalism, productivity, and sanity. But there's an added and underutilized benefit of good organization: strategizing and prioritizing. When you choose a solid organizational system, it will help you look at what you're currently working on, what is on the horizon, and what needs to happen, creating an action plan for each area of your work and life. Planning your work and working your plan will help you be proactive, rather than reactive, in your sales career. Organizing, planning, prioritizing, and identifying targets help you build momentum.

If you aren't organized:

- You don't have a comprehensive plan. This could stop you from pushing yourself to greatness.
- You experience more stress because you're trying to remember everything. Your brain might be stuffed so full that you don't have the bandwidth to creatively think about how to attack an account.

- Things can slip through the cracks. You might miss something you were supposed to follow up on or stay on top of. It reflects poorly on you if you drop the ball. In some sales careers, this can be a deal-breaker.
- You might come across as unprofessional. If you don't even look at a calendar when booking a meeting or event with a customer, it sends a negative message. The customer could think: *Is this person organized? Are they going to show up? Does she have any other customers? Is she busy? Is she successful?* You look like you're flying by the seat of your pants, and this doesn't instill trust or confidence in you.

There is one story in particular that sticks out in my mind. I worked with someone who was new to sales, overwhelmed, and practically going out of her mind with frustration. She had lots of energy but felt like she was running around all day, handling calls or issues with customers, so much so that she didn't feel like she was being productive at all. She felt like she never knew what was coming next, and that made her feel uneasy and frustrated. She also felt alone out there in the brave new world of sales.

Here are some of the things I shared with her and what I tell others facing the same challenges.

Be Proactive Versus Reactive

New salespeople often struggle with a common theme—being reactive. Whether they have a territory where accounts are spread out or close together, reps often feel like all they do is react to their day. It can sometimes feel like everything is happening at once. It can be a very overwhelming feeling.

Think about how doctor and dentist offices usually operate. If you've ever had an urgent issue, you know that the staff usually works you into the schedule that same day. They have regularly scheduled patients, but they also have built-in openings: a contingency cushion for patients with urgent issues. They have a proactive plan every day. If they filled their schedule to the brim and were surprised by every urgent issue, they wouldn't have a viable practice. They couldn't run their business that way. So, they create their daily schedule with a built-in plan for urgent patient issues.

As a smart, savvy, and organized salesperson, you need to adopt that same philosophy for your work. Be proactive in building your days around what I like to call your "priority plan." Your priority plan includes things in your day that you absolutely must accomplish. There are other goals and to-dos that you would like to accomplish, but from your priority plan, you know which things you can move to another day if something urgent comes up that you need to take care of. Your priority plan is what you use to correctly prioritize your work and accomplish those top things. Then, the next time you have some hair-on-fire situation, you're able to react on the fly, move the non-essential things around, and accomplish your priority plan items without missing a beat.

Will there be days that you still feel it's crazy and things are out of control? Yes, but it will feel less like falling out of an airplane. You'll still feel and be productive because you know how to integrate the urgent issues or problems into your priority plan.

Organization Systems

Continuity is one of the keys to successful organization. Figure out a system that works for you and stick with it. You can tweak it as you go, but starting with a solid foundation will boost your productivity immensely.

Sometimes, it takes a bit of trial and error to find the right organization system for you, and this means being tuned into the pros and cons. If you're currently putting all your information into your electronic calendar, you have no way of looking at an overview of what you're doing, targeting, and planning. Maybe you have a tiny calendar and use your phone for notes. Maybe you put your daily reminders on sticky notes and attach them to the dashboard of your car. I did that until I realized a gust of wind could ruin my day. I overhauled my planner system, and it was hugely productive.

Having an actual planner (physical or electronic) where you can put your appointments, meeting notes, strategies, and goals is extremely helpful. This is especially true for the first few years of your sales career or in times when you're feeling lost. This feeling of not being as productive as you could be often stems from lacking a system for staying organized. This is the time to think about using an electronic planner. I recommend choosing an electronic planner that lets you look at a two-page calendar of each month, where you can put appointments and larger items, as well as daily pages for you to map out appointments, meetings, cold calls, key meeting notes, and your checklist.

There are a few on the market that are actual business planners. If you would like to know the physical and electronic planners I recommend, please email me at info@stealthsales.net, and I will send the information to you.

It's also important to use an electronic calendar as a secondary place to back up your appointments, so you can use reminders to stay sharp on meeting times, conference calls, and more.

Using a planner will help you look at an overview of what your day, week, and month look like. By writing things down in your planner, you can create a roadmap of goals and/or targets to help you stay focused and on course. An electronic planner can maximize organization by achieving professionalism, keeping track of the day-to-day, and lining these up with big-picture goals and strategies.

I believe it's vital for new salespeople, or even salespeople who are struggling with productivity, to have a written planner/organization system for the first few years on the job. When you see an upcoming day that does not have a single thing written on it, girl, you've got some planning and strategizing to do.

Preparing for and Reviewing Sales Calls

One key benefit of getting organized is that it can help you make the most of each and every sales call on a big-and small-picture scale. In the beginning, it can be like training wheels to help you keep your balance and find what's working and what isn't. Using this system as you get started will ensure you're preparing properly prior to the call and reviewing your effectiveness after each call. If you're on a sales call with a senior person or your manager, it may be a bit uncomfortable, but after the call, ask some open-ended questions about their impression of the call. It's always good to get different perspectives. Remember, you have to make your sales development paramount, especially if you haven't been exposed to any formal sales training. Even if you have had formal sales training, feedback can help you rise to the top.

Very simply, Before Call Planning (BC Planning) is about determining the purpose of the meeting and what you need to bring or prepare for the call. For example, you may need to bring some literature or the product to show the customer, or a proposal. Maybe it's an informal meeting, or you could be going in to check on the equipment purchased and make sure things are going smoothly. Whatever it is, you need to identify and be clear in your mind about what you're doing there, then get it done. If you would like a sample of a BC Planning tool, you can email me at info@stealthsales.net, and I will send a sample to you.

Before walking into an account, have a Before Call Plan written down and keep it with you unless it's seared into your brain. Whether it will be a short interaction or an impromptu meeting, know who you want to see, identify your top three objectives, and know what has to be accomplished before you leave. When I had several different things that I needed to do in different areas of an account, I had my BCP written down and with me so I could draw a line through each task. That way, nothing fell through the cracks. I never worried about driving away from my account and realizing I'd neglected to take care of something. Everything was handled. When planned effectively, the BCP will provide a more efficient use of your time.

Similarly, a basic After Call Review (AC Review) is for you to do after the sales call. When you leave your account, take a few minutes to review and do a recap to make sure you reached your objectives. Check off everything you accomplished, and write down the answers to these questions:

- Was your mission accomplished?
- What are your next steps?
- Were there any surprises?
- Did you meet anyone new?
- Were there more opportunities uncovered?
- Did you get in front of the right people? Was there anything you could have done to do a better job?

BC Planning and AC Review aren't new concepts. Especially early on, these techniques help you identify what you need to accomplish; if you accomplished your goal(s); and what you could have done differently, kept the same, or done better. Keeping track of the feedback you receive as well as your goals, Before Call Plans, and After Call Reviews will help you maximize your development.

Taking Notes

Over the years, I've had the opportunity to work with people who have incredible memories and don't need to write down any notes. If you're one of those people, more power to you! For everyone else, I recommend that you write things down. Writing down key pieces of information during the call/meeting will help you put together your intel and come up with a strategic plan for your accounts and upcoming proposals. Additionally, manually writing down notes during meetings—or at least the key information shared during the meeting—allows for better eye contact, connection with the customer, and flow of conversation than putting information into your phone. If you're putting the information in your phone, your customer might think you're sending a text or checking your email.

Writing down key pieces of information will help you put together your intel and come up with a strategic plan for your accounts.

Keeping Track of the Big Picture

Being able to look at an overview of where you're spending your time will help you figure out if you need to spend less time on certain accounts and more time on others. You can then place yourself in more selling situations, making yourself more efficient.

Monthly reviews—taking a critical look back at what you've been doing and where you've spent your time—can help you identify where you may need more face-to-face time and where your time has not been as effective or productive. After you do your own productivity review, you'll have a better idea of your priorities and things you can put on the back burner.

For example, let's say you've been calling on a customer who has a fair amount of potential. You stop by weekly to check in. Every time you're there, the owner talks to you for a long time. They're already purchasing a small amount of product from you, and you know there's potential there. As you look back over last month's daily goals, you notice a trend. This customer is slowing you down. On the days you see this customer, you can't see other potential accounts and other paying customers. After your monthly review, you can change things around. Perhaps you shift your schedule so that your chatty customer becomes the last appointment for the day instead of going there first, or perhaps you start going every other week, telling the customer, "I'll see you in a couple of weeks," to manage expectations. You've now freed yourself up for your other customers and can develop more business.

It's also great to work on a rolling fourteen- to eighteen-week plan with what business you expect to put on the books in the next few days and weeks ahead. In addition to keeping you focused on where the business is and where you're aiming, it helps build your momentum and keeps you strategizing about where you're going and what you want to learn and accomplish. This way, you can be mindful about spending too much time at an account now that might not be buying until next year. Just be careful to keep your strategic plan somewhere you won't accidentally leave it with a client or the competition!

I like to keep my priority plan in a physical planner and my fourteen- to eighteen-week plan in a digital document, cross-referencing whenever new information or opportunities come along. I recommend physically writing down these plans for two reasons. First, it helps you to mentally strategize more because you're opening up your brain to potential sales opportunities while also thinking outside the box. Writing down your strategy first helps to unleash your intuition about subtle things you may have picked up on, and it helps you start to hone in and focus on exploring more potential business opportunities than if you were typing it on to a spreadsheet. I would let myself brainstorm about opportunities and write them down in a list and then go back afterward to figure out what products I'd sell to what account and what the projected timeline to get it done.

Second, writing down my strategy made me even more committed to my mission. It made me feel more committed to my strategic goal. My handwritten plan wasn't for anyone else's eyes; it was only for me and my stealth mission.

Lastly, when you achieve your goals, it feels good to physically check them off your list.

Daily Checklists

Checklists help you stay accountable to yourself, stay on top of things, and map out your plan/strategy. Writing down daily checklists also helps you learn how to prioritize. My checklists have a number by each item. They aren't necessarily listed in order, but each number lets me know the urgency and importance, from hair-on-fire swift action to a lower priority. This allows me to focus my attention where it needs to be. Properly prioritizing is essential to both your productivity and your sanity.

Keeping daily checklists in your planner not only helps you feel accomplished as you check each item off but also helps you have impeccable follow-up. By using a daily checklist, you can always keep up with items that need to be done and follow-up items. You can add them to your to-do items for your next day, week, or month. If you keep track of your checklist every day, things won't fall through the cracks, and your follow-up will be impeccable because you're constantly handling and managing that list according to priority. Furthermore, it frees your brain up to think creatively about strategies, opportunities, and how to tackle a tricky situation, customer, or problem. Instead of having all the things you need to do banging around in your head, write them down, then work your plan.

Back to that incredibly hardworking recruit I was telling you about. After she implemented the stealthy strategies I shared, she noticed a complete turnaround in the way she worked her days. She was able to channel her high energy into a proactive day, working on the things she had to respond to without letting them run her life. I didn't come up with this adage, but I like it: Routine is freedom!

The only thing it couldn't quite cure was her feeling of loneliness out there in the brave new world of sales. She had a huge territory in the middle of nowhere; she didn't know anybody in the area and had no family nearby. So, I bought her a dog. Well, I bought her a cute stuffed animal dog from the hotel gift shop where I was staying. I named him Cash. I gave it to her before I left and told her to talk to the dog whenever she got lonely. She had a great sense of humor and assured me she was going to keep that dog in the passenger seat and talk to him all day long!

11

CONNECTION AND AWARENESS

Connection and awareness are some of the most important characteristics of exceptional salespeople. And 95 percent of women can beat 95 percent of men at these any day of the week. Of course, there are many reasons for this that I won't get into because I'm only interested in what this means: most women already have the skills to be some of the most successful salespeople out there. Use connection and awareness more consciously, hone them, and make some money!

Women Are Born Connectors

In and out of sales, your success and job satisfaction depend on making connections. Whenever I meet someone and they use my name or notice something about me, they definitely get my attention. If they come across as genuine and sincere—hello! They earn even more points.

A while back, one of my close friends needed an outpatient procedure at a surgery center, so I accompanied her to help ease the nerves. We had to get there so early that we passed milk trucks on the way (only joking, kind of). As we went to check in, the nurse behind the desk was cranky. Maybe she had a lot on her mind. Maybe her coffee wasn't the way she liked it. Whatever the reason, I decided to try to bridge a connection between her and my nervous friend while she took down patient information. I thought it would be good for both of them—cheer up the nurse and help my friend relax along the way. Solid strategy.

I noticed the nurse had a Carolina Panthers logo on her lanyard. As it so happened, that was my friend's favorite team in the whole wide world. I asked the nurse if she was a big Panthers fan, she said yes, and she and my dear friend connected and started chatting away about players and the upcoming season. To keep the momentum going, I asked if she was from Charlotte. She was. That led to another minute of connection and cheering her up while relaxing my friend. When we walked away, all three of us were smiling.

If that had been a sales call, and I needed to get some contact information or start a business relationship with that nurse, this would have been a great start to a solid foundation.

Women are born connectors. We often have an uncanny ability to relate to people on a deeper level, bridge gaps, and build relationships out of thin air more easily than men. This is another reason why more women should choose sales as a career; connecting with people and building strong relationships are key ingredients to a successful sales career. Connecting also provides higher job satisfaction because when you have great relationships with customers and colleagues, it makes your days more interesting and meaningful.

The Chewing Tobacco Story

I've been fortunate enough to work with many talented people, including one particular local sales manager who was an incredible leader. I was selling for a big country music radio station, and he was my boss. He was a great boss and an incredible salesperson—a complete charmer, wonderful with people, and sharp as hell.

Connecting with people and building strong relationships are key ingredients to a successful sales career.

I asked him to go on a sales call with me because I felt like I needed some help selling to the owner of an outdoor gear store, a perfect fit for our listeners. As we were talking to the owner, I thought, *Wow! This is going really well.* The owner talked to us and opened up, sharing how he and his friends saved a little extra cash to spend on the important things: beer, chewing tobacco, and fishing.

As I methodically walked the soon-to-be advertiser down the road toward closing the sale, everything was lining up. I'd identified his advertising needs and aligned that with the strength of the station. It was going to be a perfect union. Plus, I was going to look damn good to my boss, closing the sale in front of him.

As we were having a solid "get to know me" conversation, it happened. With a subdued but proud smile on his face, the owner reached under the glass countertop and brought out a pouch of chewing tobacco. He stuck it under my boss's nose and said, "Smell this!"

My boss took a big whiff. He got a huge smile on his face and said, "Why, that smells great!"

The owner looked incredibly pleased with my boss's intelligence in understanding the delicacy he smelled. The owner began to close the pouch and put it away.

Curious and not wanting to be left out, I asked, "Can I smell that?"

Shock and awe crossed the owner's face. It seemed as though he couldn't believe I could actually understand or appreciate the complexity of what I was about to smell. He stuck the pouch under my nose, and I took a big whiff.

Without hesitating, I remarked, "I've never smelled anything like it!" with a big smile on my face. The owner grinned like a Cheshire cat. He probably thought, *She gets it!*

After that bonding moment between the three of us, I closed the sale, and he agreed to the advertising schedule. I told him I'd be back with the copy for his approval, and then we would get the spot on the air. We thanked him for his time, and as we were leaving, I almost felt like the owner was going to give us a big hug.

After the call was over, the LSM told me something that profoundly affected the way I sold. As we were walking back to the car, he asked me if I knew the greatest thing I did during that call. I was sure it was when I closed the sale, skillfully winning over the owner and wrapping up the agreement. He said no. I looked at him, confused.

He said, "It was when you asked him to let you smell that chewing tobacco. He was excited and proud about that chewing tobacco, and you made it a priority too."

What does your customer care about? Learn it, find out about it, live it, and breathe it. What are they proud of? Learn it, find out about it, live it, and breathe it.

Since that day, I've thought about why I asked to smell it. Sure, I didn't want to be left out or treated differently. I grew up with brothers, and I always wanted to be in the middle of things. But more than anything, it comes down to curiosity. Personally, I believe every female walking the planet possesses that innate gene to question and connect with people.

Which brings me to the second lesson from this experience; curiosity in sales is as important as water is to a duck. You have to be curious. Being curious about your customer will automatically lead you to understand what's important to them. Without curiosity, you can miss hundreds of subtle things that happen in a sales call. For example, in an evaluation of one of my products, a key decision-maker was speaking quietly to the person working next to him. He made a comment about something he didn't like. Watching and listening like a hawk, I piped up, asked him a question, and was able to address his issue. Without that timely response, he could have thrown a big wrench into my potential product conversion and caused me to lose the entire sale.

Awareness

After 150 years in sales and sales coaching (okay, only one hundred years), I can tell you for a fact that the setting, environment, and location—wherever you're approaching a potential customer—matters. A lot.

I went on a call with a very smart and savvy rep who knew her products inside and out. Even though she had that going for her, she'd never been taught about environment and setting the table for a conducive conversation. That was about to change.

We called on a potential account at a surgery center where we didn't even know the contact's name. We approached the front desk, which was a deep, wide counter behind a sheet of glass, and the main office area sat behind this giant front desk. We asked someone at the front desk who we should talk to, and she gave us the woman's name. She happened to be available, and the front desk person retrieved her from another area, so we could introduce ourselves and set up an appointment.

When the woman walked up, she stood in the small opening in the glass, behind that giant counter, putting what must have been eight feet between her and us. Since we were standing at the front desk where patients checked in, we were essentially standing in the waiting room; people were coming and going, and a patient's family could easily have walked through the door behind us. Between the giant counter, the hustle and bustle, and the open area where anyone could listen in, it wasn't conducive to creating a good flow of connecting conversation.

In these types of situations, you never know who could be listening and sharing your information with a competitor, or they may want to join in and inadvertently crush the flow. In my experience, it's best to always be aware of who is around, eliminate those potential roadblocks, and try to get somewhere off the beaten path when trying to build a relationship.

With the rep about to get started on the main conversation, I quickly jumped in and asked the contact if there was a place that we could all sit down and talk. She offered her office, and we followed her back. The setup was perfect, quiet and intimate, with her behind her desk and two chairs for us. Even better, I immediately noticed some volleyball trophies on display behind her and asked about them. She proudly told us about her team. I mentioned that the rep also played on a team, and there was an instant connection, like poetry in motion. After that initial bonding, the rep had a great segue into talking business with the customer. We asked her some specific questions and got an understanding of what her organization needed.

We also found out her history with her current company and where she had worked before. Knowing your contact's employment history can be important too. You may have a mutual connection from another account. This is not only good networking, but it also opens doors at another account. It was a great call.

When you talk to a potential customer, look around. Are you in a place conducive to having a substantial conversation, or is it too busy? Can you subtly move to a better spot without throwing off the mojo? If yes, then do it. If not, it may be best to see if you can get them to move to a better spot to talk. You could ask, "Is there a good place for us to talk?" or, "Where should we go to talk, so we can get out of the way?" If moving is too tricky, ask a few questions, plant a few seeds, and schedule your next meeting.

If you aren't sure your timing and location are good, there are some things you can do to take their temperature. Sometimes, the gatekeeper or frontline person can give you a feel for what's going on with the business before they bring the owner or contact to see you. Let's say you're calling on a business, and you ask the employee how everything's going. They tell you they had a flood in the storage room or that everyone is out sick, so they're understaffed, letting you know that this isn't the ideal time for the conversation you want to have. This gives you the opportunity to say, "Sorry to hear that! Please let so-and-so know I stopped by, and I will check back next week." Consideration is key.

There are definitely times when you'll take somebody's temperature, find it's too high, but still have to push through. Maybe they're always trying to stall you or put you off. Other times you may still need to push through, lay the groundwork, and have that tough conversation. As you become more seasoned with reading location, timing, situations, and environments, you'll pick up on when to continue and when to take a step back.

Women tend to already have an internal radar for all of this. We need to recognize that we already have the ability to know good timing, bad timing, and optimal timing. Let's access it, apply it, and capitalize on it! Practice that awareness you already have; it will get even better. Learn how to listen to it and make it work even better for you. The more you tap into it, the easier and more naturally it will come. Eventually, you won't even have to think about it. You'll just do it!

12

KEY PEOPLE

Decision-makers—heavy hitters—are the top key people as far as priorities on your hit list. But depending on the size of the organization, you may also come across people who aren't the final decision-makers but are crucial to you for some other reason. A key person doesn't always have power, but they usually have influence. They could have the ear of the decision-maker(s). Sometimes, when reps are full of themselves, they'll ignore the people surrounding the decision-maker. That's a huge mistake that can come back and bite them in the ass. That's why you treat everyone well; sometimes, you don't know who the key people are. Always handle people at your account with care, no matter their role.

Key people can be found in many different capacities and departments. Some key people are gatekeepers: they allow or don't allow access to decision-makers or even other key people. There are key people with influence who could be the formal or informal right hand of the decision-maker. There are key people with intel who can give you access to information to help you get further with the decision-maker. Ultimately, a key person is whoever has decision making power, access to important people, or possesses valuable information you need for that account.

Treat everyone well; sometimes, you don't know who the key people are.

On one occasion, I walked into the area where a doctor and I were going to be working and noticed a big, empty table right by the door. *Perfect!* I thought and put my book down and stepped away. Less than a minute later, a nurse walked in who often worked with that doctor. She spun around and noticed my book on the table. She said firmly, "You'd better move that! He hates having stuff on his table." She went on to explain that unless I wanted the doctor to hit the ceiling and be hot under the collar the entire day, I'd better find another spot for my book.

That nurse was absolutely key. She didn't have the power to buy my products, but she had key information about how to keep the doctor happy, and she had influence. She was wonderful. We ended up having a tremendous relationship because she always gave me the lowdown.

Key people play an important role when you're selling. A key person should be someone who works for one of your accounts and keeps you updated about what's going on within the organization. Even if it's only little tidbits, these things help you get a full picture of the organization so that you can do a better job. For example, maybe they tell you the decision-maker is a big football fan who lives and breathes the Denver Broncos. I'm not saying you should wear orange and blue to your meeting with that person, but if they recently went to a game, a great player was drafted, or you can learn something about the history of the team, you have a conversation starter.

Key people can give you access, supply you with background information, give insight to you that will help you be better at your job, and keep you updated with new information.

Sometimes, they'll even give you a heads-up on future events and the dos and don'ts of meeting with the key decision-maker.

How Do You Identify Key People?

Identifying key people can sometimes be tricky. Usually, they're the ones who have their finger on the pulse of the organization. Even though their title might not show it, these people possess information that could be very valuable to you.

A key person could be the receptionist, who gives you contact names, email addresses, and phone numbers for people you need to reach. In a cold-call situation, the key person could be the one who walks or calls back to see if the person you need to meet is available for you to introduce yourself and set up an appointment.

Once you have called on an account and built a relationship with a few of the people who work for the organization, you'll be able to tell who the key people are. The people you've built a relationship with will be able to share information and give you tips on how to sell the decision-maker. When you figure out who does and doesn't help you, it helps move things forward.

Remember, build those connections quickly and efficiently. Your main goal is to get a read on the power structure. Who are the players on the ground floor? Who are the players in the middle? Who are the ones who have the power to make or break a deal?

Flushing Out the Decision-Maker

If you're talking to someone who *seems* to be a key gatekeeper or decision-maker, you need to verify beyond a doubt that you're talking to the person with the decision-making juice. Newer reps have told me, "I sent/gave all the information to so-and-so, but they won't call or email me back." That could mean they weren't working with the power person. The person who asked for the information could have been doing it on behalf of the decision-maker and, therefore, could be blowing off the rep because they did what they were asked to do—they requested information.

Early on, it's vital to verify who you're talking to, or you could end up spinning your wheels. Even worse, while you're wasting time chasing a bunch of tennis balls that the decoy person is tossing, the person with the juice could be talking to your competitor. So, when talking to anyone you think might be a key person or the decision-maker, it's absolutely imperative that you figure out who this person is and where they fit in the power structure.

Here are a couple of my favorite ways of uncovering whether the person you're talking to has the power or not:

- "Is there anyone else we need in our conversation?"
- "When we put this thing together, will you be signing the check?" or, "Who will be signing the check?"
- "Hypothetically, when we get this deal put together, who else needs to sign off on it?"

Usually, you'll get a pretty quick reaction, such as, "Oh, no! My boss needs to okay it." If you get that reaction, you're not working with the decision-maker. You could get the reaction that the decision is made by a committee who votes on it. Maybe the board has to approve it. That's when you say, "I'd love to present this to the committee/board. How do we make that happen?"

How to Make that Connection

Try to find a basic human connection with the gatekeeper. Mention the weather, talk to them about how busy they are (even if you're not sure they're busy; people like to appear busy—it's kind of like a weird compliment), try to get them to warm up to you. Then start asking your questions.

Bridging and connecting with people is one of the most enjoyable, rewarding, and interesting parts of being in sales. Building a relationship out of thin air is challenging and a blast. You meet some great people that way. If salespeople move throughout their day and their territory only to talk about products and what their products can do for a person or organization, they're missing one of the best parts of the job.

Learning about other people—their lives, their families, their job, their hobbies and interests—is what has always made me love what I do. Being able to relate to each other outside of work, making a real human connection, has always made my job more interesting. I've always cared about my customers, and I loved hearing about what they did for fun and what they loved in their lives. When I went back for the next call, I could talk about something they were interested in prior to getting into the business side of why I was there.

I'm not suggesting you spend half an hour uncovering what people like to do, and you definitely don't want to be a windbag, but everyone has great stories, and part of life is connecting by sharing them.

Here are a few questions to crack open the door to conversation and get the ball rolling:

- What do you do when you're not running the show here?
- Did you grow up around here?
- Do you have family around here?
- Do you have any fun trips planned this summer?
- What do you have planned for the holidays?
- What do you have planned for the weekend?
- Did you do anything fun over the weekend?

All these questions open the door to build a connection. Maybe their plans include their children, a dog, or a hobby, or reorganizing their house. Maybe you also have children, a dog, or recently read a great article on reorganizing—relate to what they're sharing with you.

One time, another rep and I had to go through several people before we could talk to the head supervisor. Inside her office was a small, round meeting table with chairs in front of her desk. The table had a bouquet of balloons on it. The rep started to say something about business, but I said, "Hey, what's the scoop on those balloons?" It turned out the staff had bought her balloons because it was her birthday, and she was going to take the rest of the week off to celebrate with her family who was in town.

Learning all of that told me a couple of things. First, the rep had something to talk about the next time she visited. I reminded her to ask about how the supervisor's birthday celebration went the next time she saw her. Second, the staff liked the supervisor. This was a good sign and could mean she was a respected key decision-maker.

One snowy and freezing cold afternoon, a rep and I called on a place we thought could have potential. I'm sure most reps weren't out in that weather, and I know my companion didn't want to be either. But I told her, "You never know what great information you can discover or what key people you can stumble into on a day like today."

When we met the key person at the desk, the gatekeeper, she was super nice. I joked with her about how warm and sunny it was outside. She laughed, and I asked if she had scheduled herself to work that morning. Then we had a little fun banter between the three of us. When we told her who we were and gave her some information, she told us the names and contact information for the people we needed to meet within her organization. It was tremendous. When we thanked her and left, I told the rep, "She'll remember us, and she'll help connect you to those key people when you call next time. Keep the momentum going with her, and you'll be in good shape."

Ending the Conversation

Yes, you should relate to what the person is sharing when building a connection, but don't make it about you. No matter how interesting you think it is, remember the conversation is to bridge and connect with your key person, not tell them your life story.

There's also a difference between connecting and wasting someone's time, your time, or being a windbag. There's a fine line between building a connection and making the customer run for the hills when they see you coming. You don't want to be the person who makes them think to themselves or say to a coworker, "Oh no! I'm not going to get anything done if I talk to that rep." The customer could even be the over-talker/windbag, but they blame it on the rep to save face.

Once you have an agreement or plan, it's time to go. Never linger; you could accidentally talk yourself right out of a deal or getting more information. Your client/customer could suddenly change their mind while you're sitting there talking, or someone else could intervene and mess with the order. I watched it almost happen after my regional manager had closed an account on three big items. As he ran his mouth, the customer started to second-guess why she was buying three instead of two. We barely made it out of there without getting the order reduced.

There's a trick to getting out of those long-winded conversations with someone who wants to talk forever. Once you've covered what needs to be covered and the customer starts to talk and talk, you can say something like, "Sam, I could stay here and talk to you all day, but I need to hit the road," or, "Thank you for your time—I know you're busy/I know you have a lot on your plate. I'll see you early next week." It lets the meeting end gracefully with no hurt feelings.

Key people are access people. Their title is not nearly as important as the fact that they're key to you in some way. They have the capacity to allow or refuse access to major or minor pieces of information, to other key people, or to decision-makers. Not every key individual is going to love you or open up to you. But if you treat everyone well and connect with people where you can, key people will become obvious to you. The more you practice calling on customers, identifying key people, and learning how to cultivate those relationships, the better you'll become.

The Stalling Tactic

Sometimes, you may call on customers whose job is to stall sales reps, or at least it feels that way. You'll need to keep your internal radar up on these people. They'll run you in circles and have you chasing the proverbial ball for days. You have to figure out who those customers are and be strategic in how you eliminate their stalling tactic. The goal is to recognize stalling tactics, understand what's going on, and effectively take control of the situation and keep the ball moving progressively forward toward the sale.

The staller usually moves meetings to a later date, especially when the meeting is to go over the deal or get an answer on status. They start saying they need to run it by someone who you know isn't a decision-maker or doesn't need to be included in the process. Maybe they can't afford it but don't want to admit it. Maybe they don't have the power even though they led you to believe they did. Whatever their reason, the staller is always unavailable. They're elusive when you try to pin them down. Getting in front of them is key, followed by having an arsenal of questions to get to the bottom of the issue or issues.

I was called in to work with a rep—let's call him Tentative Tom—who had deals on the table but couldn't close any sales. It was early November, and we were fast approaching the end of the year. He still needed to hit his quota and then some. It was not looking promising. Not hitting his quota would mean curtains for him.

When I went to work with Tom, I noticed he was basically getting the runaround and being run over by his accounts. He didn't know what to do. I knew he was being stalled, and we had to work fast and blow through those blockades that were slowing the big purchases down.

At one particular account where Tentative Tom could not move the needle, he took me in to see what I could do. We met with the materials manager—let's call her Stalling Shirley. I asked some questions to confirm she was a key decision-maker. Her boss would need to sign off on the order, but the decision was left to her and one doctor.

The first thing I did was ask Stalling Shirley several questions about what was going on. I wanted to get a handle on what things were getting in the way of purchasing the equipment. As we talked, it was clear that there were four obstacles impeding progress. With this knowledge, I asked if she would purchase the equipment by early December if we handled each obstacle. The goal was to pin her down to a timeline for the purchase. We had to get a commitment for a specific time in the month that she would agree to purchase the equipment. She agreed. Tentative Tom and I got to work systematically addressing each obstacle, making an action plan, and outlining the steps.

Problem one was she had several products that were manufactured and sold by another company. She was in a bind and needed to have them repaired. She'd been trying to reach the rep but was getting no response. I took a shot with a creative approach. She would switch to our products, and we would charge her a specific amount per unit. She agreed, and I told her how she needed to ship the products to our company and how to label them. She was thrilled with the solution. One down, three to go.

The second problem was that they had multiple units of another product we sold, but some needed to be replaced due to daily use, and she didn't have time to go through ten containers to look at these units. She was vacillating about who she could get to go through and figure out which ones needed replacing. I could tell we needed to get this off her plate. I told her the rep would go through everything and report back. Then we could add the additional replacement units needed to the current order. She wouldn't have to do a thing. I asked her right then to look at her calendar and tell us when the rep could come in and look. They looked at their schedules and booked it. Two down, two to go.

Problem three was that she needed the rep to stay away the following week due to an accreditation process that was going to be happening. I looked at the rep and said, "You can stay out of here next week, right?" Tom said, "Absolutely," and we were on to problem four.

This was the tricky one. Since Stalling Shirley and one doctor were the key decision-makers, Shirley told us the rep had to get in front of the doctor and let him evaluate the products. He would only need to use it for one day. If the doctor said yes, they were good to go. The tough part was that this particular doctor was only going to be in the last week of November. That meant Tom had one day at the end of the month to get this doctor's approval. We told her Tentative Tom would be there with bells on. Tom would keep in touch with her to make sure he had all the details. As we were wrapping up, we reviewed everything we had agreed on, and Shirley was no longer stalling.

Tentative Tom was able to handle all the things Shirley needed. He got the doctor on board and was about to close the deal by early December. Tom did a great job and made his quota. Sometimes, you need to break things down and address everything in order to break the blockade and bust the customer out of the stall.

If you've ever gotten the runaround from someone, you've experienced stalling. Maybe you have children who don't want to go to bed, and they suddenly want to brush their teeth for twenty minutes, can't find a particular pair of pajamas, and want to do all sorts of other things—everything except go to bed. You could be trying to make a decision with someone who continues to drag their feet; you don't understand why they can't agree or pick something else. When you start to realize the decision-maker you're working with is putting you off or continues to throw up barriers that you have to navigate around, then you need to identify what's going on or what has changed. There are many different reasons why someone may stall. It's absolutely key that you dig down in there with questions to uncover why.

Once you know the reason or reasons they're stalling, you can make a game plan for getting around it or making it go away. You'll need to start addressing each reason and then get a commitment from them to move forward after you take care of whatever the issue is. If the issue is out of your hands, you need to continue to communicate with them and keep an eye on what's going on. Keep your hands on the wheel, but respectfully give them some room to get a handle on the issue. For example, you could be working with someone who wants to purchase your equipment, but their company recently had some internal changes with management, and the new people coming in may not support the purchase. Your decision-maker may not want to put their neck on the line and buy your products. Set up a meeting with the new leadership and strategically get everyone on the same page.

Or if a customer says, "I'll check with my (partner, accountant, administration)," be aware that this could be a brush-off move, especially if they've never mentioned them before. Don't let them brush you off. Those subtle moments set you up or delay you moving to the next step.

Remember, customers aren't stalling you for the fun of it; there are legitimate reasons that are slowing them down, and it's in everyone's best interest for you to uncover and address these barriers. Get them to agree to make the purchase once each item is addressed, pinning down a specific timeline. Summarizing and establishing a specific timeline helps keep the focus on the ultimate goal.

Depending on what you are selling, you can offer time-limited incentives to help push the deal forward. For example, if the customer/client must purchase said proposal by 5:00 p.m. the following day, it can help light the fire under your stalling client/customer. Occasionally, I would use the "fire sale" idea to create urgency and get that staller to buy. You need to be careful by being very clear about the offer. You do not want the "fire sale" to backfire. If it backfires, the customer/client could expect that "fire sale" pricing every time. That's why you must be very clear and firm that it's a one-time-only deal. If you offer fire sales every month, the impact is lost.

Before you incentivize the stalled proposal, you'll want to stack the deck in your favor. Make sure you're dealing with the decision-maker. Make sure they have the funds to buy. Make sure you've dealt with any or all objections so that nothing could come up when you offer this special deal. It needs to be doable. If you tell the customer/client that they need to purchase by 5:00 p.m. the same day and that would be hard for them, then you've sabotaged the deal before you even got started. Offer an achievable time frame that still gets the deal done and will work inside the customer/client's buying parameters.

Here's an example of this elementary-level incentivizing technique that will help you get an idea of what I'm talking about. Let's say you have a proposal on the table for $50,000.

Client/customer has been dragging their feet. You know they want your product, but you know you need to light a fire under them. You know you're dealing with the decision-maker. You know they like your product, and you know they have the funds to purchase it. The conversation could go something like this:

You: I have a special deal for you. Are you interested in hearing about it?

Customer: Yes, absolutely.

You: If this special deal is something you're interested in, would you be willing to purchase it by 5:00 p.m. today?

Customer: I can't do it by 5:00 p.m. today. My comptroller is out this afternoon, but she'll be back in the morning. I could purchase by noon tomorrow.

You: Okay, great. Do you have any questions regarding the current proposal we have on the table?

Customer: No. It looks good.

You: How would you like to get a two-for-one deal on the Y product?

Customer: That would be great. We would have four instead of two. How much is that going to cost? What's the warranty?

You: The $50,000 amount stays the same as long as the purchase is completed by high noon tomorrow. The manufacturer's warranty is the same for all of the products.

Customer: So I only need to buy the $50,000 package, and I get two more Y products at no additional charge?

You: Correct. It is a special one-time-only deal.

Customer: Done!

I'm not recommending that you give product away when a customer is stalling, but if you've tried everything else and eliminated all objections, then think about how you can incentivize your customer to move forward. There are certain times when management is more inclined to make special deals happen. Depending on your sales organization, if you are selling a new client/customer during month-end, quarter-end, or especially year-end, it might make your manager allow you to be more aggressive with incentives. Discussing everything with your manager will be the key to making sure it works for your organization.

13

NETWORKING

You never know when the people you know or work with may come in handy. That's why you must give 150 percent every day and treat people like you want to be treated.

I wish I'd kept in touch with more of the successful women I worked with throughout my sales career. I'm grateful for the many friends and connections I have, but if I could do it all again, I'd have made more of a concerted effort to keep in touch with those strong, kickass females.

I think more intentional networking would have made my path a lot smoother. It's especially important for women. Men have been networking well for years. I think it started with men's sports years ago. Women have been doing a better job, but I believe we need to make a conscious effort to keep the networking channels open. I could have done a better job keeping at least one significant female connection from everywhere I worked. Keep in mind, you're the one who needs to facilitate the connection and networking. If the other person pitches in and it's reciprocal, that's outstanding. Make sure you keep a hand in it. I believe the responsibility is on us.

Find Your Champion

At any job, you need someone who will help you go far, who promotes you to other people, and who genuinely sees your commitment to excellence. They talk you up and put you in a position to win. Having someone who recognizes your talent, effort, ethics, and smarts makes all the difference in the world.

I was fortunate to have that in my medical device job. One of my three solid bosses in medical device sales rode with me and listened to customers tell him how hard I was working and what excellent service I provided. Then, when he was promoted and went in-house, he told my customer service rep to give me whatever I requested. It was amazing. He always had my back.

Try to find your champion. It should be someone in a higher position than you in the company. As you achieve your goals, be a champion for someone else. That's what it's all about.

Leave on a Good Note

Being professional and not burning bridges is the right way to go. You never know when your paths may cross again. It's always better to keep any business relationship on the best end of the spectrum. Always take the high road, even if the other person doesn't.

I once worked for a startup company where products were going to take a while to catch on. The manager I worked for was the pits. His boss was not great either. The general manager was a good guy but clueless. I was hoping that this sales position would be a stepping stone to another company where I'd wanted to work for several years. I knew I needed to do my time and do the best job I could so that I could get to the other company. Sometimes, you have to take a couple of steps back to take a big step forward in your sales career.

When I was hired by the stellar company and gave my two weeks' notice to the startup, the general manager asked to speak with me. When I went to his big office and sat across the desk from him, I couldn't help but feel like he was proud of me because I made it to the big-time station. The startup was small, and I'd been hired by the number one station in the market. I remember getting teary-eyed and thanking him for the opportunity to work there, and I wished him well. Honestly, my tears were tears of joy! I was making it out of there alive; I was thrilled. It was the same feeling I got after surviving middle school and going on to high school. I felt relief, happiness, and downright joy.

Always leave on a good note; it will never hurt you. It will make you feel good, too. Plus, you never know when you'll need a reference.

Don't Forget to Network within Your Accounts

Networking is knowing how to capitalize on relationships in accounts and get what you need by making the customers know and feel they're valued. Having good contacts and relationships within your industry allows you to connect with others, get great information, and even gain contacts at new accounts when people eventually change jobs.

Networking is knowing how to capitalize on relationships in accounts and get what you need by making the customers know and feel they're valued.

I once worked with this phenomenal young rep. She was one of the best networkers I've ever seen. She connected with everyone she talked to and remembered them all, and she made full use of all social media platforms. At one point, she ran into a big chief operating officer (COO) for a five-hospital group. With her excellent networking skills, she got a meeting with him and two materials guys to talk about a particular machine we sold. This was a great, high-power meeting. Throughout the five hospitals, they were using several different companies' machines, and each one had its own disposable inventory in a variety of sizes. This meant they had a lot of inventory on shelves with lots of SKUs, different machines, no standardized units between hospitals, and no uniform disposable products. Staff had to know and use a bunch of different types of products. You can see where this meeting could be an incredible opportunity.

The rep had prepared impeccably and did an incredible job by going to all five accounts, identifying all of the different units and disposable SKUs, and put together this great meeting with a huge opportunity through her great networking skills. She had a proposal ready to go that would standardize the entire group of hospitals with the machines and uniform SKUs.

When we all sat down at the conference table, the chief operating officer kicked off the meeting by saying they needed to standardize all of their particular equipment in all five locations. All I could think to myself was, *Excellent! The rep has exactly what he wants!* He set the table for the rep to give him exactly what he needed. The next thing that happened surprised me. The rep said, "Let me tell you about this machine," and proceeded to talk about the equipment she brought in that was sitting in the middle of the room. She did not even acknowledge what the COO said. When she got to her proposal, I subtly brought up what the COO said he wanted. I didn't want to undercut her; I wanted to make sure she had control. But the wind was out of the sails because she could have capitalized on what he said and replied with something like, "Thank you for bringing that up, COO, because I have a proposal that addresses exactly what you requested and then some. I think you're going to be very pleased." Instead, she missed a perfect opportunity to hit it out of the park.

After the meeting, the rep and I talked about the way the meeting kicked off. She said she had in her mind how she wanted it to go and didn't pick up on what the COO said. She hadn't thought about how she should grab that momentum and run with it. She was fairly new to sales, and she was learning, but I told her she'd done a fabulous job on all the preparation, the networking to get him in that meeting, and she was going to close that deal. This was only something she could watch for next time when the customer could potentially set the table for what she's trying to sell.

Keep in Touch with Your Network

Working with many different types of people, you'll usually notice those who work hard, have a great attitude, and are extremely conscientious. From every job you leave, you should have at least one female contact, as I alluded to earlier—male if necessary, and you have a good connection—who you connected with and would want to work with again. Meet them for a coffee, do a virtual cocktail hour, be creative, and stay in touch. You never know when you may need a job reference, will be looking into a company where they work or know leadership, or need help finding new leads. Networking always pays off. Give it a chance and see how it goes.

I encourage you to schedule how you'll keep up with your network so that you keep the momentum going year after year. Add it to your calendar to reach out. Maybe you do it two to three times a year. Do not only reach out at holiday time. These relationships are important and valuable and are worth spending the time to keep up.

I challenge you to think of the people you could network with now and continue the connection on into the future. Maybe it's someone you met in a casual setting, but you could tell they're someone who's a mover and a shaker. Network with them—you have nothing to lose. The more you do it, the more you'll benefit. Networking is investing in your future.

14

QUALIFYING

Qualifying the customer is something you should do throughout your interactions with your accounts. It keeps you from getting ahead of yourself and skipping over important pieces that could throw a wrench in your sale later on. Early on with your accounts, you have to find out:

- How decisions are made
- Who has the juice
- Who needs to sign off on deals
- Who's going to help see things through
- Who needs to be in your meetings to make sure everyone's on the same page
- Whose approval is needed to get things done
- What it's going to take to get things done
- How to get buy-in from the staff
- What needs to be done

You have to qualify where the customer is in the sales process. Even if you're meeting with a customer you think is ready to buy, you still need to qualify where they are in the process. If you start your meeting and realize your customer is all over the place and not showing any buying signs, you need to back up and regroup. The last thing you want to do is start making assumptions, get too far, and then realize they're not going to buy today.

Even if you're meeting with a customer you think is ready to buy, you still need to qualify where they are in the sales process.

Let's say the customer *is* ready to buy, and all the buying signs are there. You still need to qualify some things. Unless you've done so before the meeting, you need to confirm that you're dealing with the person with the power and that you understand and address their priorities. Ask questions like:

- If I can do this, would you be willing to do that?
- If we could come through with your top two priorities, would you purchase this current equipment by the end of the month?
- Would you give us an opportunity to bring in another product to show your staff?

You need to take a step back and evaluate if they're ready to buy right now and what needs to happen to move forward. If you're working with the decision-makers, then keep asking questions. As you continue to get green lights, continue to identify and move forward with the sale. Always remember not to get too eager to close the deal. If you're too eager, you could miss some important steps, including qualifying the decision-maker, confirming specifics, prioritizing buying signs, "no" to buying signs, or ready to buy. There should be no surprises. If you've lined everything up, the buying signs are all green lights, everything is going smoothly, everyone is in agreement, but then they tell you, after you summarize, that they need to run it by their boss or a committee, you're sunk. Unfortunately, that means that you didn't do your due diligence. You didn't identify who the decision-maker or makers were; that's on you. When that happens, it's hard to back up, regroup, and bring the others into the mix. They could have a completely different set of priorities. Trust me when I say, once this happens to you, it's a wake-up call, and you won't let it happen again.

Always identify key decision-makers. Include those people in the meetings, along with the person who's helping you in the door, so no one feels left out. Protect people's egos when you're working with someone who ultimately isn't the decision-maker but has access to him or her. You could ask questions like:

- Help me understand—who do we need to sit down with?
- Once we get this proposal put together, who should we include in our meeting?
- How can we get buy-in from the people we need to make this happen?
- How do you see this proposal being purchased?
- Hypothetically, if I was able to get XYZ done, would you be willing to purchase the equipment by the end of the month?
- Help me understand what we need to do to make this happen.
- Hypothetically, if money wasn't an issue, would you be willing to move forward with this purchase?

Always try to be clear about setting expectations for your customer. If you're selling a brand-new product and there's a chance it could go on back-order, mention that to the customer so that they're prepared. When you set expectations, there are fewer negative surprises. Also, consistently summarize to close.

When you do that, it helps to make sure you and the customer are in agreement on the plan moving forward.

Uncovering the Hot Button

For years, I've been teaching sales reps about the hot button. I call it that because it's one of the most useful pieces of information you can get, and uncovering the hot button is an incredibly effective technique in sales and negotiation.

Any time a customer sits down with you, they want something, too. It's up to you to figure out or uncover what that something is. What they want, their reason for sitting down with you—that's their hot button. Once you know a customer's hot button, you can understand and explain how your product fits what they're fired up about. Here's an example of how uncovering someone's hot button could look in action and why it's vital to the sales process.

A new rep and I had an appointment with the acting director of supply chain. Let's call him Elusive Edward. Elusive Edward was a significant player and a key decision-maker. Prior to our meeting, I talked to the rep about identifying the hot buttons and decided this acting director of supply chain would be a good place to teach her how to do this.

Little did I know, this was going to be an interesting journey. Elusive Edward told us about the significant openings in management at the account. They needed a new director of supply chain and an OR supervisor. He said they were in the process of hiring for both positions. I started by asking him different questions to figure out what fired him up or what the priorities were for the hospital. I asked him about past purchase decision-making and other background information. He answered the questions, but I was still trying to figure out what his hot button was. What was going to get him to let us come back in the door again? He wasn't providing anything that made me stop and think, *Aha! There's his hot button!*

The whole meeting felt ridiculous. Trying to pull information out of him was futile; I was getting nowhere. I knew he had a reason for sitting down with us, but I couldn't uncover it. I'd asked everything in my arsenal to flush him out, but nothing worked. So, I stood up, the rep stood up, and we thanked him for his time. As we turned around to leave, he asked, "What does XYZ hospital have down the street?" I thought, *Are you freaking kidding me? It's that simple? His facility doesn't want to be seen as being behind in technology. He wants to keep up with the Joneses. Of course, he does! I can't believe my questions missed identifying that competitive hot button.* Sometimes you may find or realize that your customer doesn't even know what their hot button is until you ask a question that brings it to light.

Fortunately, the competing account had our equipment, and it was fairly new. When the rep told him about the other account, Elusive Edward said that when the new OR supervisor was hired, they would take a look at our equipment.

You need to keep digging for the hot button. When I got fed up thinking he wasn't going to tell us, it was our getting up to leave that finally did it. Remember, at some point, they're going to tell you what their hot button is, even if it's in a subtle way, so have your radar up. They could even tell you right out of the gate. It could come up at the beginning of the call. You could be thinking it's something else but realize that's not it. Follow where they take you. Incorporate it into what you're asking or talking about. What's important to the customer damn sure better be important to you.

After telling that story to another new rep, she asked, "What would you say if the other hospital had the competition's equipment, not yours? What would you tell the account then?" In that case, maybe you have a newer technology available or additional product(s) that you could sell this account. Maybe they'd look at something that the competition doesn't sell, and only you sell. If you're working with that other account, too, you could mention you have an open dialogue with the competitive account, and you're talking about some other options. You could say you don't want to get into a lot of specifics, so you're respectful of both accounts.

Keep It to Yourself

Not getting into specifics is the most respectful tactic when talking about multiple accounts, but there are other reasons too. Keep in mind that the person you're talking to could be friends with your competition, and he could tell your competition what you're doing. It's always important to play your cards close to your chest. Don't share what you're working on because you never know who someone could tell. If you talked about the plans of another competitive account, the account could think, *Is she going to share information about our purchases?* They wouldn't want you broadcasting their information either.

When I was selling, I always kept what I was doing under wraps. I looked at it like I was playing poker; I never let on what I was holding in my hand. I wasn't going to tell accounts or outsiders if I had a full house, a royal flush, or zilch. I wasn't going to tell them anything. Because I didn't know who they were. Were they my friend or foe? Were they asking out of mere curiosity, or were they asking because they want to tell somebody, or for some other reason? Since I didn't know if they would burn the hell out of me and tell my competition, or accidentally hurt me, or were just curious, I always thought it was wiser to be cagey and kept my information and strategy to myself. I never wanted my competition to see me coming. It always paid off for me to move with stealth.

Even if it's unintentional, you never know who could inadvertently hurt your business by repeating something to the wrong person. It's better to stay off the radar. Be generic and vague in your answers. If they push the question, you can divert and ask them what they have going on for the day. For example, if they ask where you're going, you might say, "Oh gosh, I have so much going on. What do you have going today?" If they continue to ask, and you've already answered in a generic way, then you could ask, "What makes you ask that question?" Then you may get to the root of why they're asking. It could be harmless, or they may change topics. Either way, keep your cards close, so no one can see what you're holding or learn your ultimate strategy. This ensures what you have going is safe.

Once I was working with a new rep, and we were talking with some staff at an account in the nurse's lounge. A doctor came in for coffee and started speaking with us. After introducing ourselves, he asked all sorts of rapid-fire questions to the new rep about her job and territory. As I watched this unfold, I wondered what this doctor wanted.

Then he asked, "How much do you guys make?"

Quickly, I said, "Whoa, doc. What makes you ask that question?" I wanted the rep to stop answering all these intrusive questions, so I could find out the doctor's motivation.

He said, "My nephew wants to work for your company. He's trying to get a job there."

Then I started asking him the questions. I said, "That's great. Everyone has different territories and a lot of different variables. Do you know who your nephew is talking to?"

I told him I'd pass along his nephew's information to the manager but wasn't sure if there were any open sales positions. He was happy with that and went on his merry way.

This can happen in your personal life too. Sometimes, people want to know too much information that's none of their business. Try it on anybody. If you realize someone is asking too many questions or getting too much in your business, answer a question with a question and redirect them, or ask, "What makes you ask that question?" Be stealthy. It works. You'll find that you won't give away any information you don't want to.

Women are beautifully primed for both of these skills: understanding what people are fired up about and keeping our information under wraps. Uncovering a hot button takes skillful questioning, listening, and reading people's energy—all things most women can do far better than most men without even trying. Keeping your own information/strategy quiet through subtle redirecting is something most of us have had to practice throughout our lives. By understanding these skills as dynamite sales tools, honing them, and using them more consciously, I believe women have an enormous upper hand when it comes to stealthy sales, so let's use it to fatten our bank accounts!

15

NEGOTIATION

Nuanced and complex, negotiation has a lot of moving parts. Especially when starting out, many women feel overwhelmed by how much there is to know, which I think is unfortunate because we are damn good negotiators when we have the confidence to give it a shot. My goal here is not to try to give a comprehensive review of advanced negotiation techniques. Instead, I want to give you enough basic tools so that you feel comfortable trying them. After all, the best way to get better at negotiating is practice!

Getting More Horsepower

My parents told me if I wanted a car, I needed to sell my horse, Steele. I'd earned money from many hours of odd jobs and babysitting, but I also needed the money I'd get from selling Steele.

I loved that horse so much, but my parents felt I wasn't going to have a lot of time to spend with him with my newfound freedom and the fact that I played a lot of sports. Back in the day, when you wanted to sell anything, you put it in the want ads. You put in your home phone number, what you were selling, and the price. So, Steele went into the want ads: *Looking for a good home.* I was hoping some young rider would love him as much as I did.

I got some calls and showed him to a couple of different potential buyers. There was one man with three daughters—I like to think of the father's name as Mr. Squatty—who took a huge interest in Steele. The young girls seemed to love Steele, and I was excited for him to receive all that love and attention. He deserved it.

We bought Steele for a whopping $375, including his saddle, saddle pad, and bridle. We were selling him and all the other gear I'd acquired for $275 because I'd put a few years on him. We were getting close to having everything handled for the sale of Steele to that nice family, but then Mr. Squatty called one evening. He told me we needed to come down on the price. He said Steele had a scar on his side, so he wanted to pay significantly less. This threw me. It hit me emotionally at first. It was hard enough to come to terms with letting go of Steele, and then the man wanted a cheaper price because he was "damaged." Steele wasn't an object. He was my buddy whom I loved dearly. At the same time, the money from selling Steele was helping me buy my car. I needed the money. I was very conflicted. I told Mr. Squatty I'd talk to my dad, and we'd be in touch.

When I told my dad, I thought his head was going to fly off his body. I know now that my dad knew this guy was trying to jerk us around. Every time Mr. Squatty had seen Steele, he had seen the scar, so it wasn't some new development. My dad told me that I was going to handle the conversation with the man and that we were not dropping our price. If Mr. Squatty didn't want to pay it, then we were done talking to him about buying Steele.

When I called the man back, my hands, my head, and my whole body broke out in a cold sweat. I wanted Steele to be with those cute little girls, but I knew my dad was right. When I relayed the message that we were not budging on the price, he said they still wanted Steele. Whew! I breathed a sigh of relief and happiness.

The day they came to pick Steele up, my dad, brother, and I were at the barn. I loaded Steele in the one-horse trailer with tears running down my face. But I knew he was going to have a good home.

Steele always took good care of me. As they were rolling away, Steele, in all his glory, gave me a final salute and a big laugh. He lifted his tail and ripped the loudest, longest fart I've ever heard in my life. He made me laugh and cry all at the same time. I loved that guy.

Learning to hold my ground on price was an important lesson my dad taught me. I'm grateful Steele ended up in their home with the little girls, but even if he hadn't, I wouldn't have minded keeping him around a little longer.

Let's break some of this down. When the man called trying to lower the price on Steele, I was suddenly in a negotiation. At sixteen years old, I had no idea what I was doing, but I knew I needed to talk to my dad. This was absolutely and unconsciously a brilliant negotiating move on my part. You never want to drop your price the first time a buyer suggests it. Swat that away like a fly. Instead, step back and be strategic. Tell the buyer you need to double-check something (or check with someone, whatever fits your scenario) before agreeing to anything.

Telling Mr. Squatty that we'd call him back was another strategic move, unbeknownst to me. Be the caller, not the callee. There's more power in controlling the next chess move. This applies to outside strict negotiations as well. It drives me crazy when I hear a rep say, "Let me know on that," or, "Give me a call when blah-blah-blah." The rep is telling the customer to call and follow up with him. The rep is the one who's going to make the money, so the onus is on the rep, not the customer. You need to be the caller. You need to follow up. Take the wheel and drive.

You must be in control. If you put it on the buyer, they may not remember. Plus, it's probably not a priority to them. You're the one who needs to follow up every time. Instead of saying, "Let me know," you could say, "Should I touch base with you at the end of the week or early next week?" or suggest some follow-up you'll do. You always take the lead. You'll be in control of staying on top of your follow-up and next encounter.

If I were coaching my sixteen-year-old self through that negotiation, I'd tell her that before you step away, you need to uncover everything the buyer wants. If you come back ready to negotiate and work something out, the other party may throw something else at you. So, it's important for you to make sure you know what they're going to ask for, get them to prioritize, and decide with your boss (or your dad, in this case) what makes sense. There are a ton of variables, so it's important to remember that this is a general overview of the negotiation process.

Uncovering what the buyer wants without committing to anything is similar to getting a birthday list from your child. To avoid spoiling your child and finding yourself in financial ruin, you need them to tell you which one or two things they want the most. Once you get that information, you know what their priorities are. Obviously, when they hand you their list, you're not going to say, "Okay, little Susie. You can have the firetruck, the beach toys, and the doctor kit." Because what do you think the next words out of little Susie's mouth will be? That's right; little Susie will ask for more. That's what a customer or buyer would do too. In both cases, you step away to figure out what makes sense. You know it would be a bad move to agree to Susie's gifts right there on the spot because you not only need to make sure you can find those items but also you need to make sure you can afford them.

Now, take this example and apply it to a customer. You need to find out what they have on their proverbial birthday list without agreeing to anything outright. You get everything on the table, so you know exactly what you're dealing with. The next step is to figuratively step away, so you can take a look at what makes sense, and if you're ready for Negotiation 102, you might also look at the benefits to you and or your company. You may not have the power to agree to what the customer wants and need to talk it over with your boss first. Maybe your boss wants you to negotiate for the customer to commit to buying or evaluating more products, a longer contract, or a shorter timeline on the purchase; there are tons of options and variables depending on the situation. But in all of them, including for a clueless sixteen-year-old selling her beloved horse, an important step in the process is taking a step back to regroup and figure out your negotiation strategy.

The First (and Only) Townhouse

I was doing well selling radio advertising in Denver. I knew this was where I wanted to spend my life and decided it was time to invest in property.

I was renting from a friend who told me about some new townhouses near her place. At the time, the economy was not doing well, and the townhouse company was trying to unload the last few units.

Armed with that strategic nugget of information, I spoke to the man in charge of selling the remaining units. He didn't seem to have the power to do anything. He said he did, but there was something about him that suggested otherwise. He showed me around, and I found the unit I wanted. The price was $85,000. I told him I'd pay $70,000 for it. He acted like I'd insulted him, his mother, and his father before telling him he had an ugly baby. You know what I mean; he was mad. I asked him to please mention my offer to his superiors. I'm positive he didn't take my offer anywhere but the garbage can.

Day after day, I wore the man down. I kept going back in to see if the unit was still available. Then I put earnest money down, had my credit checked, job checked out, boss called, the works. Finally, I was a viable buyer. He was not keen on working with me, but there was no other interest or offer. I was the only game in town. My guess is that his superiors told him he had to sell the unit to me.

When I thought everything was coming up roses, I got a call from the measly mouse man. He called me at work late in the day. He said that the company had only approved the sale for $75,000 instead of $70,000, so I had to pay another $5,000 or the deal was off.

I was mad, and it seemed like everything was slowing down around me. I felt like this guy was jerking me around, so I decided to call his bluff. I believed his people had told him to take the deal, but because I was a thorn in his side, he wanted to jerk me around a bit more. He was probably pissed I was going to get my way.

I told him, "Five thousand dollars to me is huge, and five thousand dollars to your corporation is a drop in the bucket. If they want five thousand more, then tell them I don't want it." It was bone-crushing to say that, but I knew I had to call his bluff. He told me he'd have to speak to his people.

Within the hour, he called back, and I had my townhouse! Years later, I sold it for $12,000 more than I paid for it. Sweet profit!

Once again, I need to make it crystal clear that this is an extremely perfunctory overview of a highly complex and involved topic of negotiating. If you're brand new to negotiation, my hope is that these tips will encourage you to dip your toe in the water. After all, when it comes to negotiation, the courage to practice is the best tool I can give you.

Offering Less

When you're the buyer, you can take a shot at purchasing something for less than the given price. In those situations, it benefits the seller too, but you'll benefit more. A couple of years ago, I wanted a little end table to put in our newly redecorated family room. One day, I walked into a store and found the perfect little black end table. It was $279. I liked it, but I felt like $279 was too much to spend after we'd bought a new sectional sofa, flat-screen TV, coffee table, and chair. The budget had been exhausted. I left the store but kept thinking about that perfectly sized table.

A couple of days later, I went back. After looking at the table again, I noticed a few minor scratches on the top; they were not monumental but noticeable. The way I wanted to use the table, no one would notice them but me. There was a lovely woman behind the counter, so I went up to talk to her about the table. I mentioned noticing a few little scratches on it and wanted to know if she had another table in the back. She did not. I walked her over to the table and pointed out the scratches. I told her I liked it, but those scratches didn't make me want to pay $279. I asked her if there was something we could do. In my head, I decided that I was willing to pay $200.

As it turned out, she was the owner. Jackpot! I was dealing with the person who had the power to decide. I asked her what she would be willing to do on the price of the table. In a heartbeat, she said she could order a new one, scratch-free, or sell the floor model to me for $199. I countered and said I'd purchase the table for $180.

Her first reaction was, "Oh no. I can't sell it for that."

"Okay," I said, "but I'd really like that table."

She asked if I could write a check. Fortunately, I had my checkbook with me. When I said yes, I could write a check, she said she'd do it. I wrote her a check, put the little end table in my car, and smiled all the way home. I love that little table.

The lesson for you, Stealth reader, is it never hurts to ask. The worst they can do is say no. But they may give you a counteroffer or take a percentage off. It's up to you to figure out whether their offer makes sense for you. I think the owner wanted to move some of her merchandise; the table had a few little scratches, and she had a viable buyer. You may be too young to know this, but there's an old saying that a bird in the hand is worth two in the bush. If you've got a viable buyer in your hand, don't go looking for two other buyers walking around the store because they might just be lookie-loos.

When you try negotiating, remember to slow down and look objectively at the situation. Knowing that the townhouse company wanted to unload the units gave me an advantage. They had probably done extremely well selling all the other units at list price, but they were losing money while the few units left had no buyers. I believed it was almost a fire sale type of situation. That's good for the buyer. When it came time to stand my ground, I knew I needed to walk away in order to get what I wanted—or not. The less emotionally attached you are, the better you'll do, whether you get what you want or not.

When you try negotiating, remember to slow down and look objectively at the situation.

Try negotiating when you're buying a bigger item or last year's model. I always start with a lower price for any big purchase, such as a townhouse or car. Frequently, I get a no right out of the gate, but I treat that as the start of the conversation. Usually, there are variables you and the seller can work with. Maybe you buy the current year's model since the brand-new versions are about to hit the market/dealership. Maybe you work something out with the seller regarding warranties or upgrades. However, I do not negotiate for any type of service. I once heard about someone trying to negotiate the price on services at a nail salon. That's ridiculous.

I've always looked at negotiation like a sport. The more you practice, the better you get. Remember to stay objective, take a step back, and then try it. What do you have to lose? In fact, you could keep a little more cash in your pocket or make more money.

16

CUSTOMER CONVERSATIONS

When I first started selling, I didn't understand the cadence of a sales call. If I happened to do it correctly, I was completely unaware. But over the years, I finally learned because it paid off. I noticed that when I tuned in to each customer's personality and customized my pitch, it always led to a better interaction. Some customers wanted the information short and sweet, some wanted more detail, and some weren't even sure what they wanted. Checking in during the call would always help aim me in the correct direction.

Over the years of selling and coaching others, I've watched many incredibly smart people be oblivious to the cadence of the call. The great news is that once you start keying in and paying attention to the customer's cadence, you'll notice a subtle but definite shift in your calls and, ultimately, in your opportunities. You'll be running with the big dogs at that point.

Sometimes, reps—especially new reps—try to accommodate the customer by answering a question at lightning speed, even though they could have gotten more information if they'd allowed for a slower cadence. Even when you're excited or have been rushing around all day, when the customer's cadence is slow, or they process differently than your last customer, it's up to you to slow down and get more valuable information. Take a deep breath and have the patience to allow things to unfold naturally, and you may uncover some nugget of information that can help you sell to your customer.

If a rep is talking intelligently but at lightning speed, a customer could feel like they're being bulldozed and become suspicious that the rep is glossing over important information or hiding something. Or perhaps the rep is flying through and thinking the customer understands when the customer is actually off in la-la land thinking about what they're planning to do for the weekend. Take a breath and check in. To gauge the right cadence on a call, check in with your customer verbally and mentally.

You could ask:

- Does that make sense?
- Does that sound good?
- How do we get the staff on board with this?

Mentally take note of the following:

- Are they looking at you in the face?
- Are their arms crossed/uncrossed?
- Do they look comfortable/uncomfortable?
- Are they leaning forward/back? (Leaning forward means they're interested and engaged. If they're leaning back, they aren't there yet; they're exhausted, having a rough day, or not interested.)
- How long are their responses? (Short, irritated answers *could* mean they're ready to kick you out.)

Keep in mind that your own voice and body language are key to cadence and sales in general. I remember working with one rep who was talking to a customer and turned their body to the side and leaned against the wall. The customer was standing there looking at the side of the rep. After the call, I explained how that was a shut-down-the-conversation move.

Matching the customer's cadence not only demonstrates respect for their time and how they process but also is one of the main factors that contribute to high-quality relationships and customers feeling like you get it. One of my favorite examples of successfully matching cadence happened when I was training a brand-spanking-new rep—and I mean brand new—who had been on the job for less than a month. As we pulled into the parking lot for our next meeting, her phone rang. I could hear the customer, let's call her Marge, saying that she didn't want to meet with us, even though the meeting was scheduled to start in less than fifteen minutes.

She said, "I already bought all new equipment, so I don't need anything."

I whispered to the rep, "Tell her it's only an introduction, and we won't take more than ten minutes."

After Marge agreed, the rep hung up, and I told her we had to get in front of this battle-ax.

"We need to know if she's a key decision-maker and what capital equipment she just purchased. If we can't do that in ten minutes, then we shouldn't be in this line of work."

It's good to throw down the gauntlet and challenge yourself every damn day; this was ours. We gave ourselves ten minutes to figure out whether we had a shot at her business.

As we walked into Marge's office, she pointed at two chairs that had been pulled away from the other two desks so that the three of us were sitting in a small triangle. Right off the bat, I said we would be there for ten minutes as we promised. During the conversation, I kept a sharp eye on the time. As I matched the right cadence for her, we asked targeted questions to quickly extract some specifics about whether she had the juice and exactly what equipment she purchased. Even though she'd said that we had nothing to talk about since she'd already bought all new equipment, it turned out she'd bought a few of only one type of device. She had plenty of other old, dated equipment that needed to be upgraded, and guess what? Yep! We could supply her with everything she needed. Furthermore, she was a key decision-maker. Within five minutes, we had accomplished our goals and uncovered tremendous opportunity—and we had five minutes left!

After planting a few seeds about some ideas for her business, we set up the next meeting. This is something you should always do when you have a tricky time getting in front of somebody. Ask something like, "What day next week works best for you? What time?" Make sure you look at your calendar so you don't overbook yourself or look like you have nothing scheduled or planned. If you blankly look up to the sky like you have no future commitments, you look like a lame rep, and it sends the message that nobody is likely buying your products.

At ten minutes on the dot, like Cinderella, we stood up and proceeded to leave. Since we'd matched her cadence, respected her time, and kept our promise, she followed us out, continuing to talk to us as we walked out into the corridor. It was beautiful. You should always leave the customer wanting more, and we definitely left her wanting to meet with the rep again.

After our meeting, the rep and I devised a strategic plan to get her account on the map with our gear. The rep did an excellent job and earned her business. It was successful customer cadence from the start.

The Ask-It-Back Technique

At one point, I was selling radio advertising for the biggest radio station in the market, which happened to be a country music station. Back then, country music didn't have the popularity it has now. In fact, people often refused to admit that they listened to it. But from our market data, we knew there were many people who ran organizations and had discretionary income who listened to our country music station. Selling the station's format to advertisers would sometimes uncover people in high-level positions who didn't want to admit they loved country music.

While selling to this particular group, I learned a fantastic tool, and it works far beyond that particular demographic of country-music-listening audience. When a potential advertiser said something ridiculous like, "Nobody listens to country music," instead of arguing, saying, "Of course they do," or, "I have statistics that show differently," I'd simply say the statement back as a question. "Nobody listens to country music?" Then I'd wait. Right before my eyes and ears, I'd hear the advertiser handle their initial objection. I heard my clients say things like, "Well, *I* listen to country music, but I'm probably one of only a few who listen." That's when I'd bring out the statistics and address the unfounded objection. It was and is extremely effective.

This technique of repeating a statement back like a question reminds me of the "Bend and Snap" technique from the movie *Legally Blonde*. Reese Witherspoon's character, Elle, teaches Jennifer Coolidge's character, Paulette, how to get the attention of a UPS guy she has the hots for. The Bend and Snap works every time!

Check it out for yourself. For example, say you and a friend are talking about a movie, and your friend comments that nobody saw that movie. You say, "Nobody saw that movie?" Like magic, you'll hear your friend say something like, "Well, *I* didn't see it and heard it wasn't that good, but I'm sure people saw it."

Once you've taken it for a ride a few times and seen how effective it is, you'll see how useful it could be for getting customers to handle their objections. You keep the conversation going, and your customer is more likely to be receptive to your numbers or other information since they've already addressed their own doubt.

Kind of stealthy, don't you think?

Active Agreement

After training reps in this skill for years, I created the term Active Agreement to help pinpoint the dual goal and balancing act of encouraging comfort and information sharing while simultaneously identifying and honing in on the information that is important.

When practicing Active Agreement, start with one or more open-ended questions until the other person, often the customer, begins to take the wheel. As they talk, you're smiling, nodding your head, and asking more open-ended questions. Your body language is relaxed, open, and engaged: your arms are uncrossed, body and face relaxed, and your expressions are following and responding to what the other person is saying. These actions encourage opening up and more information sharing.

Your goal with Active Agreement is to make the other person comfortable, so they'll talk more. The more comfortable they are with you, the more they will tell you. The better you understand them, the better job you can do. By using this skill, you're building a bridge based on authentic connection, and both you and the customer benefit. Remember, Active Agreement can be used with anyone, not only the decision-maker.

Your goal with Active Agreement is to make the other person comfortable, so they'll talk more. The more comfortable they are with you, the more they will tell you.

Active Agreement allows the customer to take the conversation where they want it to go. Maybe they want to talk about the dynamics in the workplace or their frustrations or what is going well. No matter what direction they want to go, creating an open, comfortable relationship strengthens your connection with the individual and can also open the door to opportunity. All sorts of things can come up in these conversations. It's up to you, the person doing the Active Agreement, to key in on the important information—the signal—and let go of the unimportant—the noise.

For example, a customer might share how they're dealing with a difficult situation or dynamic. As you key in on this important piece of information, the customer is helping you to be more cognizant of a fragile work environment. Similarly, if the customer is having difficulty with another department in the account, that could potentially affect an order you're trying to close. In that case, you need to dig deeper and uncover what needs to happen to get the order placed.

I recommend trying Active Agreement on a friend. Try asking a few open-ended questions to uncover information, and then focus further to get the specifics. It's important to practice because it's a real skill to be able to balance both aspects of Active Agreement at the same time; you want to create momentum in the conversation while simultaneously identifying and focusing on key information.

You might ask:

- Is there anything going on that I need to know about?
- Seems like the place is a well-oiled machine—is that right?
- Are there any landmines I need to know about, so I can do a great job for you?

You're trying to identify as much information as possible, such as:

- Who are the players?
- Is there opportunity?
- Is there opportunity next week? Month? Year?
- How big/small is the opportunity?

In a conversation, here's how this might look:

Customer: "I'm going to go on sabbatical for the next two months."
You: "Oh, that's fantastic! Where are you going?"
Customer: "I'll be on a bike trip in Italy."
You: "What are they going to do without you?"
Customer: "So-and-so is handling X," or, "We're not making any capital purchase decisions while I'm gone."

Remember, the term is *Active* Agreement and not "enthusiastic," "passive," or "open-ended" agreement. That's because there's a certain rhythm to it. If you're overly enthusiastic, it can come across as contrived or like you're cheering on instead of actively participating. You want to actively encourage the conversation without enthusiastically running over whomever you're talking to, scaring them because you're right next to them in the conversation, or wandering aimlessly as you ask open-ended questions without focusing on a particular direction.

Remember that sales is a noble profession. One of the essential pieces to this tool is that there needs to be an authentic connection and genuine interest by the rep. Active Agreement doesn't work if the connection isn't genuine, or you're trying to game the customer while you're getting them to talk. You, the rep, aren't leading a lamb to slaughter. Instead, you're providing an authentic format to allow the person to feel comfortable enough to share.

I always try to demonstrate Active Agreement to any rep I coach. Sometimes, the customer will dive deep into information I believe would not normally be shared. I always make sure to explain to the rep that they are in the circle of trust. Whatever was shared needs to go in the vault. She trusted you, and if you respect and honor that trust, she will appreciate that. If you choose to repeat it, you'll destroy what you started to build with her. You have an opportunity to do business here if you play your cards right and protect that confidence.

While this tool can always be honed, I believe women tend to be incredibly skilled and experienced at drawing people out. Active Agreement keeps the momentum moving and affords you a better understanding of the shoes in which that person is walking.

Planting the Seed and More: Why Women Rock at Sales

"Planting the seed" can mean many different things in sales, but I'm going to talk about two general kinds of planting the seed: planting the seed of an idea and planting the seed of doubt. In general, planting the seed is a stealthy way of introducing a thought or idea that registers with the customer subtly and over time.

Planting the seed is a great sales technique for anyone, but I think women both tend to be better at it and can benefit more from it. For women, it can be tricky to directly state something to the customer. From an early age, through school, and on into the workplace where boys and men are seen as direct, assertive, and strong leaders, women engaged in the exact same behaviors are called bossy, unfeminine, and bitches. However, that doesn't mean we lie down and let the guys take charge; instead, it means that most of us have gotten good at an essential life and sales skill: planting the seed. Women have mastered this and done it intelligently for years. We sell this way; men can only hope to. In fact, a male rep was once telling me how over the moon he was about this hot-off-the-presses sales technique he learned—Make it Their Idea. Unimpressed, I told him women have been doing that for years.

Instead of blatantly stating something, you can plant the seed and let the customer ponder something and let it germinate. In a beautiful moment, the customer may end up flipping it around and saying your thought or idea—the seed—was their idea. Mission accomplished!

For a gorgeous example of this, look no further than the movie *My Big Fat Greek Wedding*. The big family owns and runs several businesses together, and the lead, Toula, doesn't want to work at her parents' restaurant anymore. Instead, she is interested in using her new computer and career skills to work at her aunt's travel agency. Her aunt Voula and mother Maria support this but fear that Gus, the father, may not. So, they pull off a classic Planting the Seed maneuver:

Maria: "So, Voula. How is business?"

Aunt Voula: "Oh, woe to me. Business is bad."

Gus: "What's the matter? What's happened? Do you need money?"

Maria: "No, what she means is that, with the two businesses, she suffers."

Gus: "She suffers?"

Maria: "She suffers. She has to be at the travel agency alone, all day, because everybody else needs to be working at the big dry-cleaning store."

Aunt Voula: "That's right. I make Taki go to the dry-cleaner store, and now I've no time with him."

Gus: "So, send Angelo or Nikki to the travel agency, and you be with Taki at the dry cleaner."

Aunt Voula: "That . . . would be good . . ."
Maria: "That would be no good. Because . . . neither Angelo nor Nikki knows how to use the computer. That's why that no work."
Gus: "Computer . . . Ah! I have your answer. Toula will go to the travel agency, and you send Nikki here to work for us."
Aunt Voula: "I can't believe that. Wonderful!"

Masterful! But how does this look in real life? Once, I was working with a rep who had been talking to someone in the materials department at an account but had not gotten very far. The account had reached out and said they needed one of a particular product we sold. The title of the person we were meeting with said it all—director of purchasing. She had the juice and the knowledge of the dollars available.

When we went to her office, we saw the materials guy who had been stalling the new rep. We were early for our meeting, so after he walked us to the director's office and was hanging out in the doorway, I asked him some questions to get a better understanding of what products they currently had and where we had more opportunity to sell them ours.

Once the director arrived and the materials person bowed out, we asked her some questions about her product of interest. We confirmed that they currently had three and asked if they wanted another one because they were doing more with that product or because they were upgrading an old one. She said they were getting busier and needed one more.

As the rep talked about the new technology, I planted a seed. I mentioned offhandedly that it could come in handy to standardize and upgrade all three of their units. After all, having everything uniform would help the staff, and there wouldn't be an issue with one department wanting the new technology and no one wanting to use the old equipment; everything would be new and the same. I then planted another seed about whether it could be helpful to streamline the disposable products as well, so they'd have less inventory and avoid multiple SKU numbers.

We talked about doing some sort of trade-in/purchase on the two devices with old technology and purchase of the additional device and disposable products that went with all three. The fresh information we obtained from the materials person was coming in handy, and the discussion went extremely well. We identified some other opportunities to upgrade their old technology since the account was becoming a lot busier and had higher demand on their current dated products.

As we were wrapping up, the director asked for a quote for all three of the devices plus disposable pricing. The planted seed was coming to fruition. We discussed the timeline and the next meeting to go over the proposal. We scheduled it, thanked her for her time, and left.

Planting a thought or idea is one way to plant the seed, and as you can see, it's extremely useful. But you can also plant the seed of doubt. I've never been one to disparage the competition. I think it's tacky when sales reps do that. Plus, it usually backfires; the customer could already be using the competitive product and it's working fine, or maybe the customer's nephew works for that company. Those reps can lose ground with customers when they say disparaging remarks.

Planting the seed of doubt can help you position your product or service without running those risks or compromising your integrity. I'd rather position my product in a way that highlights the differences without saying, "Well, their products are cheaply made." To plant the seed of doubt, I'd rather say something like, "We are the only ones in the market to carry this or offer that . . ."

If your customer brings up the competition, think of it as a time to prove you know your stuff. Instead of making sweeping generalizations like some inadequate reps, take a few specifics and highlight the differences in a positive yet definitive way:

"My understanding is that Such-and-Such Company does not have XYZ Technology," or if you know their service isn't great, "How has their service been on that product?" By handling that carefully, you can build up your customer's knowledge of what the competition lacks and differentiate your products. Plant the seed of doubt with your impeccable knowledge of your own and your competition's products.

If your competition does not have integrity, or they're saying things that aren't true about your product or theirs, maintain your position on the high road. Show the customer your literature or whatever you need to do to underscore the correct information you're providing. Recommend they ask for proof of the BS the competition is slinging. You're going to run into unsavory competitors, so be prepared. Plant that seed of doubt and be ready for anything.

I remember selling a solid medical device product. My competition's product was good too. However, I knew most of my competition had a huge hole in their game: They were terrible with service. They had bad follow-up, wouldn't show up when there was a problem with the equipment, and wouldn't check in on customers. Customers were sharing that with me, and they were often surprised to see me and get whatever they needed handled right away.

My customers kept telling me that when they bought equipment, the rep never showed up to unpack, provide training and refreshers on the equipment, or anything at all until it was time to sell to the customer again. Even the sales rep I'd replaced at my own company had operated that way. I knew it was time to change the game, and it would benefit the customer. It was a total gap in the competition's game, and I knew I could fill it and leave them in the dust.

Instead of telling my new customers that I was going to do a great job and give them the best service ever, I told them my goal every day was to out-service my competition. And that's what

I did. I never said I was going to do it that way. I said my goal was to do it. Underpromise, overdeliver is a great philosophy to live by in sales. As time passed, my customers ended up telling me what exceptional service I provided. They even told my competition about the great job I was doing. I planted the seed, but they made it flourish after I proved myself.

Here's an example of how this method of planting the seed triumphs over being too blatant. A new rep for a competitive company was going around my territory, telling the staff and doctors at my accounts that I sold subpar products, and he was going to be a much better rep than me. Weeks later, he walked into an account two hours late for what he wanted to do there. When he wanted to go do it anyway, the tough-ass OR supervisor walked him to where I was working with other staff, pointed to me, and said, "The early bird gets the worm." The guy lasted less than two years.

My customers saw me show up when they needed me and when they didn't need me, and I always made sure to leave things better than I found them. I made an effort to build trust in my accounts. One of the toughest, most stubborn customers I converted told one of my competitors, "Lori is like a jack-in-the-box. You never know when she's going to show up. She's always here when we need her and even when we don't."

Would they have noticed this without my planting the seed? Who knows? What I do know is that I drew their attention to my competition's biggest weakness and simultaneously turned it into my biggest strength.

Planting the seed is a way to open the door to the customer mulling something over and then potentially asking more about it. Maybe it's the seed of an idea—an opportunity, a product, even a promotion—or maybe it's the seed of doubt about your competitors—their product, service, or some other strength you have over them. Planting the seed is a stealth skill that women excel at, so use it to make some money!

Clearing the Air: Uncomfortable Conversations

What do you do when you feel something isn't quite right with the customer/account? Let's say you've done a good job with your account, but something feels off. For example, there was an account I'd been calling on since it was under construction, and they bought all of my products. A few years later, it was time for them to upgrade their equipment. I knew they were going to look at other companies, but I also knew I'd done an excellent job with customer service and staying on top of everything.

I'd been working with the account's facility manager for a couple of years at that point. She had been a nurse there until the previous facility manager had left. She was quiet and serious and often tricky to read, but I started to notice that the last few times I'd spoken with her, something felt off. I couldn't put my finger on it, but I knew something wasn't right. I wanted to clear the air, and I wanted to find out what the problem was. I knew I couldn't make it better if I didn't know what was getting in the way.

I knew my customer loved Snickers bars, so I went to a convenience store and bought the largest Snickers bar I could find. Fortunately, at that particular time in history, the Mars candy company made a bar you could practically play baseball with, it was so large. Only joking, but it was probably a foot long.

Since I was tight with the staff and had great access, I walked into the facility manager's office and found her working behind her big desk. Carefully, I placed the large Snickers bar on her desk and took a step back. She looked up with a weird look on her face. I said, "I'm not sure what I did or what I goofed up on, but I'm hoping you'll tell me. I value our business relationship too much to let it fall apart. I thought the Snickers bar would crack you up." She smiled and ended up sharing her thoughts with me. She said I'd come on too strong when we spoke a while back, and she didn't like that. She felt frustrated with me. I apologized profusely and thanked her for sharing. I told her I'd learn from this and that I truly appreciated her feedback.

There are two lessons here. First, I didn't make excuses. At the time, my competitor was trying to get their business. I was on high alert, and it probably showed. One of my most trusted docs had told me my newest competitor in town had been telling people he was going to knock me off my pedestal. Funny, I never felt like I was on any pedestal. If I had been, it would have been covered in grit, grime, blood, sweat, and tears, dammit. Second, when men push, they get more room, more runway to do what they want to do. Pushy women are considered bitchy and get very little leeway.

That day, I took initiative, was thoughtful in my approach, and was able to clear the air with her. She could have shut me down or told me everything was fine and shut me out. She could have purchased my competitor's equipment. But she stepped up and told me the truth. I don't know if that was comfortable for her, but I was incredibly grateful that she shared her perception. I've always been more inclined to open up the conversation, even though it's difficult. She needed to be heard. I needed to learn. I wanted to get to the bottom of the issue because I think it could have cost me the business if I hadn't gotten her to tell me what she was thinking.

I did end up getting the business, but it was frustrating at times with the competition annoyingly close, and I'm sure the facility manager could feel that from me. I had to learn to temper my intensity, or I was going to keep coming off in a way that would be counterintuitive to earning anyone's business.

People often think they might make things worse by laying everything out on the table. However, even though it can be excruciatingly uncomfortable, I truly believe that doing this is vital to success. You have to be able to get the customer to talk, even if it's something they're upset about. It's good practice too.

You have to learn how to successfully have these conversations. Clearing the air is extremely important. Women are especially good at facilitating difficult conversations, dealing with the issue, and leaving the person feeling good afterward. We can tell when something is off, and we want to figure things out and ultimately make them better.

Of course, you have to be strategic about how you bring up a tough subject. You don't have to buy anyone a Snickers bar, but you may need to extend the olive branch to encourage dialogue. Being aware of egos, feelings, and histories doesn't hurt either. Look at things from their point of view. If done carefully and respectfully, this type of uncomfortable conversation can take the relationship to an even higher level. It's about understanding where they're coming from. Try to figure out the answers to the following questions:

- What needs to change?
- What can they tell me, so I can do a better job next time?
- Why is it hard for them to tell me this information?
- How can I fix this issue or perception they have?

If you can get someone to open up, you may not agree with what they share with you, but you never argue. Accept their feedback, and learn from it. If you put it all on yourself, it will open up the dialogue—kind of like that classic breakup line, "It's not you, it's me." You're saving face for the person you don't want to hurt.

I could have thought, *She would never say that to a guy, that he's pushy. A male would be looked at as a go-getter, whereas a female is pushy and aggressive.* Instead, I chose to focus on how she opened up to me and had the trust to tell me what she thought. I knew that was key.

It's possible that your customer is way off in what they're telling you. Say, for example, they're upset with your company or a previous rep or manager—something you have no control over. Once they make a statement like that, you could say something like, "I'm sorry. That is not the way I do things or how our company does things. I'm sorry that happened. Moving forward, I will prove that to you. It may take time for you to see this, but I will give you my best." Then make damn sure you give them your best. Prove it.

I always tried to leave my customer with a smile on their face, or even better, laughing. This keeps the door propped open for the next time you're there. Maya Angelou said, "People won't remember what you said or did, they will remember how you made them feel." That's what I'm talking about. When you have to discuss something difficult or uncomfortable, you want to make sure you hear what your customer shares. If you focus on listening, acknowledging, and leaving them feeling good (if possible), you're one step closer to building a stronger working relationship.

I remember working with this one particular customer: a battle-ax who'd been around for at least a hundred years. She never smiled or laughed. She always looked like her underwear was too tight. The one thing I knew about her was that she ran a tight ship. I knew if I was going to sell anything to that account, I had to win her over.

One day, I went in, sucked it up, and told her I knew she was well respected and knew everything that was going on. I told her I wanted to help her and be an asset. I asked her if she could share anything with me, so I could do a better job and help her and her staff. Shockingly (only joking), she brought some things to my attention. Most of them were ridiculous, but I never challenged her. I listened and thanked her very much for sharing.

After that, she was nicer to me. Letting her vent was the best thing I could have done. In all fairness, she never exactly warmed up to me, but I was able to learn more about the nuances of that account because she shared with me. Mission accomplished.

Uncomfortable conversations can be about price increases, issues with products, interpersonal issues with customers or colleagues—all sorts of things. Remember to get the issue on the table, own up to what they're upset about, try to leave them feeling good, and build a stronger working relationship. Tough conversations aren't necessarily going to be the most fun part of your day, but they need to happen and will likely go more smoothly if you initiate them. In general, people will appreciate that you respect them enough to be open and honest, take feedback, and clear the air. Initiating the difficult conversation also gives you control over the time, place, and your mindset going in, so you aren't caught off guard. If you frame it well, you can also learn a whole lot more about whoever you're talking to by getting the uncomfortable stuff on the table.

17

KNOW AND UNDERSTAND YOUR CUSTOMER

Name Calling

When was the last time someone you just met called you by your name? Do you remember how it made you feel? It always catches my attention, and I almost do a double take. I believe there's a lot of power in using someone's name.

When you're working to connect with people, make an effort to let their name register with you and then use it. Paying attention to someone's name, company name, and correct pronunciation is key. Remember to say their name with a smile on your face—yes, you have to watch your face!

Even when you understand the importance of these things, it can be tough to put into practice. Here are some tips and tricks I've collected over the years to cultivate this crucially important skill for connecting.

I once heard an idea about how to remember somebody's name. In your mind, picture the side of a white barn, then paint the person's name on the barn in red. This has been very effective for me. I also make an effort to use a person's name several times the first time I meet them. It helps solidify their name in my mind. Then, when I'm back in my car, out of sight, I jot their name down and maybe a couple things I learned about them. Then I have a great conversation starter for next time.

If you miss the person's name the first time you meet, try to catch it right then and there, saying, "I'm sorry, I didn't catch your name." If you've read a person's or company's name but aren't sure how to pronounce it, write it down phonetically and practice it. Put the internet to use if you need to. I've said things like, "How are you, young man?" no matter the age or, "How's everything going, fella?" to avoid using their name. This has a flip side, though, because some men still say "sweetheart," "honey," or "babe" when they don't know, or don't try to know, a woman's name. I hate this. When in the presence of those Neanderthals, I call them the same name right back. It actually gets most of them to stop, or they learn my name because they hear how condescending those words sound. Some don't, so I continue to call them sweetheart or whatever, even though I took the time to learn their names.

I also try to use humor when I get a name wrong. For example, when they've corrected me, or someone else piped up, I've said, "I knew that! I just want to make sure you knew it!" It usually gets a chuckle, and then we move on. As with all humor, it depends on how forgiving your audience is. If you're around a bunch of crabapples, they're probably not going to joke with you, so it's best to ask or apologize. You can also wait until somebody else says the name or discreetly ask the person's name once you're out of earshot. You may even call someone the wrong name because they remind you of someone. It's okay to tell them, "Oh my gosh, you remind me of my favorite teacher, friend, neighbor . . ."

When you meet somebody, it helps to remember one thing, especially if it's one thing they want you to know about themselves. It could be something personal or maybe something they like or like to do. Whatever they emphasize or tell you, make a "note to self" and use it next time you speak with them.

I once got into a conversation with a guy who worked in the grocery store I frequented about where he was from. The next time I saw him, I didn't remember his name, but I remembered he was from the Lone Star State, so I started calling him Texas. He loved it. He was very proud of where he was from. I don't recommend that you call people the name of the place they're from, but it helps to remember one thing about them. You can always bring it up to start the next conversation.

Stealth Sales Starters

This next technique may sound a bit contrived, but if you understand the genuine components of it, it works. I've found throughout my life that if you start interactions with a positive comment, gratitude, or funny one-liner, you'll enjoy your interactions more, and you'll build connections faster. I like to call them the Stealth Sales Starters. Here are some examples of each.

Positive comment/genuine compliment

- This building is beautiful. When did you renovate?
- I appreciate your effort in getting this meeting scheduled. How's everything been going?
- Your staff runs this place like a well-oiled machine. How did you build such a solid team?
- Is there something new or interesting that you've been working on?

Gratitude

- Thank you for talking with me. I know you have a lot on your plate.

- Thanks for spending a few minutes with us. We just wanted to follow up.
- Thank you for taking the time to discuss the issues you've been having.

Humor

- If it's hot out: I'm glad it's so cool and comfortable today. It would be miserable if it was really hot!
- If it's during a blizzard: "I'm glad it's not snowing! That would be awful!"

Then, to further the connection: "Are you from here? Doesn't it seem unusually hot/cold/humid/whatever?" You're trying to get engagement from the other person. I've found it helps to lighten the mood no matter who you're talking to. Sometimes, bringing in a little levity helps you build a small bridge. And be sure to keep smiling, so they know you're joking—especially when you don't know them well!

In my experience, nine times out of ten, using any of these three openers will start a connection. Sometimes, you may end up needing to use a few openers or even all three categories to get something started. Watch for the other person beginning to engage.

Since you're reading this, I know you want to take this concept out for a spin—so do it! The next time you're out and about, try connecting by using a Stealth Sales Starter or come up with your own. You've got this!

Women are Natural Observers

Have you ever unloaded part of the dishwasher, only to realize the dishes were dirty? Yuck! When you've done it once, it probably won't happen again. The next time you open the dishwasher to unload it, you'll have your senses on high alert. Does it smell like freshly washed dishes? Did the soap dissolve? Is there a little puddle of water on the upside-down glasses or bowls? Do the dishes look clean? Now, obviously, if you live alone, this is a moot point. But when you live with others, and everybody helps, sometimes nobody turns on the dishwasher at night and then you could easily put away dirty dishes.

Women are natural observers, constantly noticing things a lot of men miss. We have a heightened awareness. That's one of our strongest tools. Think about the last time you walked through a parking lot in an enclosed area. My guess is there were a ton of different things you were observing to make sure you got to your car safely. If anyone else was in the parking lot, you probably kept a sharp eye on that individual. My point is this: As women, we already have this great sales tool built in. Being observant as a salesperson is absolutely key.

Here's another example. You walk into a restaurant around noon. You realize you could pick any table you want and sit there. Translation: Nobody is eating at the restaurant, and if they are, they're sitting at the corner table reading something—and it's the owner/manager. It may not smell like anything good is cooking, and no one even comes out to seat you. This place could have some major issues, but follow me on this journey for a moment.

Now, you also know their dinner business is great; sometimes, it's even hard to get a table. You also know the business has a couple of other locations and that those do well with both lunch and dinner. You observed in the past year that more competition has opened in the area and think that could be affecting their lunch business.

Also, what have you noticed about the role of the staff? Are you observing them being enthusiastic, productive, pitching in, and doing anything they can to help make the restaurant look good and be successful? All of this is information to keep in mind when you talk to the owner.

Being sales observant is the ability to put the things you notice in your arsenal to use when you need them. To continue with the above example, as you work with your restaurant customer, you continually notice that every time a certain employee is close, the customer seems more agitated. You lock that away in your arsenal. A few weeks later, you find out that the employee is the customer's brother-in-law. You learn that he's lazy and doesn't do his job. You didn't ask about what you noticed, but you sensed it. Now, there's confirmation, and you know to steer clear of the brother-in-law. You would never want to invite him into a conversation with your customer.

Being sales observant is the ability to put the things you notice in your arsenal to use when you need them.

If you were selling advertising to that customer, you'd want to ask questions about where she would want to increase her business. Your guess would probably be right that lunch was not doing well, but you need to hear everything from the customer to assess and decide if you can help with your product.

This next story exemplifies *not* being observant. A sales rep I was coaching wanted to introduce me to his customer, so we went into the account to say hello. As we walked around, he spotted the customer. She saw him as she was speed-walking, almost running, to a hair-on-fire situation. She gave him a look that I interpreted as: "You're not going to try to talk to me right now, are you?" He held up his hand as though to signal her to stop. That did it! She said, "I can't talk to you now!" He looked oblivious to what was going on—the opposite of what a great rep would do.

An observant rep—and, I think, most women—would not have tried to stop her. A simple, "I'll see you later, keep up the good work!" or, "Looks like you have your hands full; hang in there," would show that you get it and would probably earn some big points with her.

By recognizing the timing isn't good, a great rep would take that hair-on-fire situation, move her own agenda to the back burner, and support the customer in the throes of an urgent situation. By choosing a compassionate route based on the circumstances, the rep builds credibility and subtle points with her customer. She'll be able to approach the customer at a better time, with her previous smart, compassionate choice intact. This male rep's choice was to satisfy his agenda, either oblivious to or not caring about the customer's situation. He wanted what he wanted. But gauging the customer's reaction to his hand up in the air, it was apparent that he came across as inconsiderate and oblivious. This sent the message to the customer that his agenda was more important than her situation.

Women are like a force in nature, consciously or unconsciously knowing what to do to survive. We are acutely aware of noticing subtle nuances that help us gauge approachability in any given environment. Often unconsciously, we take in and size up the whole picture—the look on somebody's face, the environment, attitude, approachable/not approachable, frustration, anger, happiness—and ingest it all. Because we've learned to survive by being constantly aware of the small things, being adaptable, and being flexible, we can survive and thrive in ever-changing environments. Customers will always gravitate toward sales reps like us, especially when we learn to consciously put our observations to good use.

We are conditioned by society and family to be overly aware of everyone else. While there are times this can get in our own way, sales is not one of them. In fact, it makes women inherently excellent salespeople.

Below are some ways to consciously tune in to your observations and become even more sales observant:

- Look around. What do you notice? Is there something you can talk about to build a connection or bridge with the client/customer?
  - There was a photograph of a teenage boy in full high school football gear on a customer's credenza. Knowing the rep that I was with played football in college, I thought it could be a quick connection, so I asked, "Who is the football player?" I wasn't sure if it was her child or grandchild, so I let her tell us; the conversation could have gone sideways if I asked if it was her grandchild and it was her child. The rep and customer connected right out of the gate. By the time we got to talking about the business we needed to cover, they were able to connect on a whole different level.
- Do you have something in common with this person?
  - Maybe she's wearing the same top you bought recently, or the photo in her office shows a football game, and you went to the same school she did. Bingo! Talk about that first.
- Is it a good time?
  - Even if you have an appointment, it may not be a good time. Ask if you're not sure: "Is this a good time? Would Friday work better for you?" If this customer usually stalls you, don't give them that opportunity.

Using your observations to notice ways you can connect and keep connecting with your customers is key. Notice everything. This will prepare you for the next time you talk with them. It's easy to ask about something you previously talked about at the next meeting. I've always enjoyed my job more when I had the opportunity to connect with people, learn more about them, and share experiences. I believe it provides more depth and job satisfaction.

A keen sense of awareness and observation will allow you to do a better job, and tuning in to it on a conscious level can open doors. Remember, women already have this built in! We need to keep tuning in to and honing our sales observing skills.

Reading the Room

As a salesperson, you need to be aware of not only your client/customer but also what's going on around you. Reading the room means both being aware of the environment and being socially aware. I believe that women have a tremendous internal radar for reading the room. The following are a few stories to underscore the importance of this skill.

I once worked with a rep who was a laid-back and relaxed guy. We went into one of his accounts, and he told me we needed to walk all the way to the back, which meant going down several hallways and an office area to get to our destination. As I was walking through the restricted access area with the rep solidly behind me, I heard a sassy, I'm-going-to-kick-her-in-the-ass woman's voice say, "Where does she think she's going?" Of course, I stopped. The rep backpedaled and told her who we were and who we were going to see. She gave me the once-over and let us continue on.

In retrospect, I think I should've made sure the rep led the way instead of me. He was the one they recognized, not me. Ultimately, there was no harm done, but being aware would have drastically improved this situation. If the rep had known this woman was a little nasty, he would have known that he should be in front of me.

Here's something to think about. Let's say that you're the first to arrive at a big meeting. There's a long conference table in the room. You never, I repeat, *do not ever,* sit at the head of the table. Depending on how many people are attending the meeting, it may be best to sit toward the middle or wait to choose your seat. Put your things down away from the table, check anything you need to check, and then remain standing until everyone is there or people start sitting down.

One day, I was working in the OR and needed to speak to one of my orthopedic surgeons. As I walked up to the scrub sink area, I realized two of my top surgeons were back-to-back, scrubbing in for their individual cases. There was complete silence except for the running water and scrubbing. You could have cut the tension with a knife. I realized at that moment that walking up to one before the other could be extremely detrimental to me. It was a no-win situation. There were big egos involved, and I had to be very careful. These two men had broken up their practice a couple of years prior, so their relationship, or lack thereof, was like a bad divorce. Fortunately, neither one had laid eyes on me, so I made a quick U-turn and walked away without a trace—a stealthy retreat. I spoke with both surgeons separately later that day, which meant that neither would feel slighted. Paying attention will always pay off.

Another scenario in which it's important to read the room is when you get into a customer's office, and they don't offer you a seat. You can tell they're busy even though you have an appointment. Unless they're a customer who constantly stalls you, your best move is to read what's going on and say to them, "Let's set up a time to talk later this week," or, "I'd love to follow up with you regarding such-and-such. Does Friday work for you?" If they offer you a seat, you're on borrowed time.

Read the room. Do they look slammed? Irritated? Frustrated? Do they need to let off a little steam? Ask a couple of questions and figure out what's going on. Maybe they need a little levity; maybe they need some compassion, or maybe they're frustrated with something they're working on. Whatever it is, find out what's going on, help if possible, or set up another time to meet with them. You'll earn points because you've been considerate and aware.

18

BEST PRACTICES

If you're looking to get out of a sales rut, starting out in sales, coming back to your career after a break, or upping your game, these are some useful tidbits I've collected over the years of selling and coaching. Hopefully, they'll help inspire you enough to get you revved up and back out there!

Do Things Differently

- Figure out where the hole is in your competition's game.
- Going the extra mile means going above and beyond taking care of your customer and your company. Sales reps who consistently go over and above will always be irreplaceable.
- Call on accounts when it's not a popular time to go. I used to work on the weekends and well into the evening. It set me apart from other reps, helped my accounts, and customers appreciated that I was committed.
- Meet customers face-to-face. Sometimes, new reps complain they never hear anything back after emailing. I think that's because you lose the ability to connect to and read a customer by communicating through email instead of

talking in person. Plus, if what you need to talk about is dicey, even more reason to have a face-to-face conversation. Show up.

- Always be detail-oriented. It's imperative you consistently have impeccable follow-up on *everything*—not just product purchases. When you say you're going to do something—do it.

Speak with Ease and Authority

Working with new young reps, I've found it helps to coach them on strategic pausing. It's good to take a breath before letting the words come out of your mouth, avoiding a knee-jerk reaction. When someone's new, they can be fast to answer a question or respond to something, and that takes them backward instead of forward in the conversation. It's always best to pause, collect your thoughts, and say something properly. I've heard new reps come out with some negative or damaging lines while meaning the exact opposite. It doesn't mean that you can't recover from it, but it's better to prevent something like that from happening by slowing down, taking a breath, and collecting your thoughts before blurting out something to give a quick response. It will help you in the long run.

How you position and frame things to a customer is extremely important. Choosing the right words and framing your point well will help with the communication flow. The last thing you want to do is position something poorly, have the conversation go off the rails, or give the wrong impression. Choose your words carefully and frame things so that you're clear, concise, and positive.

End Meetings with the Next One in Mind

Summarize at the end of every meeting. This technique is useful to clarify what's been agreed on, outline the action steps, and set up the next meeting. Setting up your next interaction will help you keep the momentum going. Plus, the customer may add something else to what needs to be done or remember something more they need to say.

Ask Open-Ended/Probing Questions

Sometimes before starting a meeting, I say, "Is there anything you'd like to discuss before we start our meeting?" or, "Before we get started, is there anything you would like to address?" I like this soft-shoe approach instead of asking, "So, why are we here?" or, "Are there any issues or problems?" Those aren't productive conversation starters. They're duds.

Remember, if you're sitting down with a customer, they want something too. Maybe you can get them to open up in the beginning, so you can customize your pitch even more. Maybe they have an issue with your company or product. In that case, it's best to get it out in the open before launching into trying to sell something else. Always deal with that before getting into your agenda, even if it's to say, "Let me look into that and find out what's going on." Then you make it a priority.

If you get a sense that something else is going on, you could casually ask, "What's the scoop with blah-blah-blah? Is there something we are missing here?" Your goal is to open the door and find out what's going on, deal with it, and move everything forward.

When you're talking to the customer about anything to do with your company, make sure you use the pronouns "us" and "we," not "they" and "them." You aren't an outsider to your company. It helps you to take more ownership for your company and conveys that you're representing your company. I remember listening to a rep talking about an issue the account was having with a product he sold: "Well, they don't put enough into development." He was slamming his company, talking about who he represented as though he didn't work there. I recommend saying something like, "We are really working on that issue, and it's a priority to us (as long as that is true.) Thank you for sharing that information with me."

Never Compare

One time, I made a mess of a situation thinking I was being strategic. I was attempting to sway a hundred-year-old crotchety doctor to use one of my products. He was one of those people who resented change. This great strategy came to me: tell him about another doctor who was like the Tiger Woods of the operating room. Unfortunately, that spur-of-the-moment idea blew up in my face; as soon as I said it, he stomped off. An incredibly kind and astute nurse buddy of mine, who I'm still friends with today, walked up and asked what I said to the surgeon.

I said, "I told him Dr. Woods loved my product, and he should try it because he'll love it too."

The nurse smiled kindly, like an adult would smile at a small child declaring something ridiculous, clearly not wanting to crush the child's spirit.

She said, "Never tell a doctor that another doctor likes something. It means death to your sale."

Well, she wasn't that dramatic, but the point is: Never tell a customer they're going to like it because so-and-so likes it.

Carpe Diem

When selling radio ads, I had a hell of a time getting to see one particular car dealer. He owned several dealerships and was incredibly elusive to all who wanted to sell him something. I happened to have the best country radio station in the land, and I was damned determined to get him on our air. Finally, after what seemed like forever, I made it to the promised land: his office. Standing across the desk from the man himself, I knew, this was it. *I have to close him today! I'm selling him an advertising schedule on my spectacular station before I leave his office.* As we discussed what he did and didn't want if he bought a schedule from me, I asked if I could use his phone. He said yes. While standing in front of him, I called my boss to get him to approve the rate for the ads I was about to sell. Our incredibly sharp sales assistant answered the phone and said the boss wasn't around. Knowing I wasn't getting back in front of the owner, I acted like the sales assistant had the power to say yes or no to the deal. She played along, and I closed the sale. Later that day, my boss was blown away that I got that car dealer on the air. Carpe diem—seize the day.

Listen Past the Answer

Many times, people will tell you how to sell them or what it's going to take to sell them; you need to listen closely and listen past the answer. Sometimes, little gold nuggets of information are buried in their conversation or their response to a question from you. If you stay quiet and pay attention, your radar should notice those subtleties that will make all the difference in the world. Pay close attention and ask great follow-up questions when they need a prompt.

Never Assume Anything

I was once working with a rep who had been doing a great job with her accounts. We walked into one and saw one of her key people. She looked happy to see Blair and made a beeline toward us.

As she arrived, she looked at Blair and said, "I need a quote for a new tower."

Before Blair could say anything, I asked, "How many towers do you need?"

She paused, tilted her head to the side, and said, "Actually, I need two towers."

When we walked away, Blair was smiling.

She said, "What just happened? You just doubled the dollars."

I said, "Never assume anything. Sometimes, you have to throw something out there to see what sticks to the wall. She could have responded to my question by saying she only needed one. She didn't. It was easy to see you've been doing a great job in this account, and it just paid off."

Connect the Departments in Your Accounts

I once told my audience of sales reps that one of the best things they could do is to connect different departments in their larger accounts. By doing this, you become a key strategic player in the decision-making process. You could end up being privy to information you normally wouldn't have access to, all because you're the bridge between departments. When people rely on you and you help connect the dots, you can end up being essential in the flow of communication and potentially the purchase of your products. Each department in an account has some reason why your product makes sense. You could share that information with all the different departments while laying the groundwork for the purchase.

Become Part of the Family

Every industry has its own badge of honor, the values or experiences that make you an insider. My first month in medical device sales, this tall, tough, salty nurse came up to me after a visually challenging surgery.

Unsolicited, she walked up to me and said, "You're going to do just fine in medical sales. You didn't pass out or kiss the doctor's ass; you're going to be just fine." She knew I was new. I loved the hell out of that nurse.

Another time, I was with several of my nurses when we saw a male rep up at the control desk.

One of the nurses said, "Oh, there's the suit."

I piped up and said, "Hey! I'm a suit."

The other nurses said, "No, you're not a suit; you're one of us."

That was one of the greatest compliments I ever got. Show up for your accounts, earn their respect, and become part of the family.

19

STAY HUMBLE

It's important to remember that respecting yourself and having confidence doesn't mean thinking that you've got it all figured out. Coachability is one of the most important characteristics of an exceptional salesperson. Think about professional athletes; they could have all the talent in the world, but they still use coaches to help them hone their athletic ability and be the best they can be. If an athlete got all bent out of shape, took it personally, or refused to implement a suggestion every time they were shown how they could be doing better, they'd have a terrible reputation and wouldn't last long on that professional team.

Throughout my career, I've been taught many things to help me become even better. Although I'd like to tell you those lessons only came early in my sales career, that's not the case. Being coachable is a prerequisite to growing and learning, no matter what you do or how long you've been doing it. It doesn't mean that the critique is always right, but I do believe you need to listen and implement what you can to get even better.

There are many different ways of doing things in sales. Hearing and being open to constructive criticism or pointers from someone more experienced can always help you learn what you can do to be better. If they're taking the time to give you feedback, acknowledge it and utilize it to the best of your ability. It may have been difficult for them to share; keep that in mind too. Always thank someone for sharing feedback with you, whether it was good or bad. It's always been important for me to listen to constructive criticism and then do something to better myself. I believe this is an important characteristic that we all need to possess and embrace.

As a sales coach, I know the importance of being coachable. When I've worked with salespeople who think they have it all figured out—and usually shared that with me—ten out of ten times, they ended up being the ones who needed coaching the most.

One of the greatest leaders I'd ever worked with (let's call him Jack) and I were working on a plan for bringing my coaching services into his organization. He'd asked me to put together some information about myself, so he could pass it on to his boss. So, I sent him something I'd been using for a couple of years.

After he brought me on board and I was working with his people, during a great moment-of-truth in a conversation, he told me that he never forwarded my information on to his boss. He said it was bad. In fact, I think he said it was terrible. He said it wasn't written well and was disappointing. He felt the literature didn't represent me well at all. Now, granted, I'd had other people look at it and double-check it for me, but he didn't like it, and he wrote extremely well. I took his comments to heart. I thanked him and said I appreciated his feedback.

Then, I looked for a kickass editor. I spoke to one of my most trusted confidantes, Forrest, who recommended an incredible editor he'd met a few months prior. I reached out to her and started a wonderful relationship. She was a tremendous editor who helped me with all of my company's written information. She was the perfect person for the job. Any significant emails, written letters, and reports were done top-shelf. It took my coaching business to an entirely different level.

There are many ways to adapt and overcome your weaknesses. I believe women adapt and overcome much. We are able to make decisive change when we know our challenges.

I coached one rep who told me about a big opportunity at a busy surgery center. He kept saying how badly he wanted the deal, but after asking him some questions, I realized he hadn't even gotten in front of the doctors to show them the equipment. I recommended an email he could send that night to try to salvage a deal at the last minute. The doctors and the facility manager were meeting that next morning to discuss the future equipment decision. Obviously, it was extremely time sensitive.

The next morning, the first thing I asked him was how the email turned out. Did he hear anything back from the doctors? Completely unabashed, he told me that he had taken his son to Chuck E. Cheese and hadn't sent the email. It was clear that he had never put in the effort to get this deal. I started to wonder if he even had the doctors' email addresses.

As we went on a few calls that day, it was clear that he wasn't at all coachable. I mentioned some things he was doing that were going to kill his credibility. He did them again. He didn't care about what I was advising him. When he did it one more time, I told him to run me by my hotel. When he asked what I needed, I told him I was picking up my luggage, and I needed to go to the airport; we were done. He didn't make his quota and didn't last.

Feedback can be tough to hear, especially when it's negative. But it's worse to continue without knowing what you're doing wrong and even worse when people around you realize you can't be taught. Never assume that you have it all figured out. Approach feedback with gratitude, and keep getting better every single day.

Under-the-Radar PR

I'm a firm believer in strategically doing stealth public relations (PR) for yourself. This type of under-the-radar PR should never be confused with bragging. Instead, it should be consistent and subtle, like a drip campaign—the perfect tool in a Stealth Salesperson's toolbox. Under-the-radar PR is pointing out all the great things you're doing for your company and your customers in the right times, doses, and places. When done correctly, under-the-radar PR allows leadership and customers to realize exactly how much you go above and beyond the call of duty. It reinforces the right message in their perception of you and your potential.

That said, I've learned a lot by stepping into some big steamy piles of—well, you know what I'm saying. The following is a great example of how *not* to do PR for yourself.

While trying to get a customer to see things my way, I brought up a good deed I'd done for them. It was not the first time I'd reminded her about what I'd done. But this time, it was not pretty. I turned magenta while my customer ripped my head off in front of several of her coworkers. After banging my head on the steering wheel for a bit, my AC Review with myself went something like this:

Me: Why the hell did you bring up that good thing you did? Again? For the twentieth time?
Self: I wanted her to agree with me since I took care of them.
Me: I think the reverse happened.
Self: Ya think?
Me: I will only mention my good deeds to the right person or people, and only once.
Self: Good idea. Continue to let them know all the great things you're doing and taking care of, but for heaven's sakes, be *subtle!*
Me: Roger that.

There's a big difference between PR and bragging ad nauseam about your accomplishments.

In contrast, an example of good PR is slipping in a story or comment from someone that shows you in a positive light. For example, you run into an associate from a previous job, and they tell the person you're with how lucky they are to be working with you. At some point in the near future, you mention the encounter to someone (or several people) in a position of leadership. It may or may not help you, but it reinforces the right message and makes them think about your potential.

Solid PR also helps if someone tries to undermine you or take credit for your work. One saleswoman I worked with, a consummate professional who had done a fantastic job with her accounts, told me she worked with a male counterpart who took advantage of her goodwill. He went on a call with her, and even though she had prepared impeccably for the customer meeting, he pushed her into letting him run the call. It didn't go well. Later, the customer even told her that she should have done the call.

"I didn't like that guy and didn't trust him. He didn't know our account like you do."

These types of situations will happen, and having a solid foundation set with your PR is incredibly helpful when they do. When someone swoops in and tries to take credit for your work, they could get shut down—*hard*.

Like this rep, I've also had men take credit for my work. Once, I was called in by leadership to turn around a bad situation. The company was going to lose a significant deal for over $600,000. I turned it around, and we got the deal. Several months later, in a big leadership meeting, the regional sales manager, who didn't care for my strong backbone and my . . . let's call it my bullshit meter . . . credited his rep friend, who was going to get an additional deal with that account.

Right there in the meeting, in front of all the other leaders, the President/GM and the VP both lambasted the RSM bastard as soon as he started making it sound like the rep had made this business happen. Both men gave the RSM a swift figurative smack upside the head and reminded him that had I not turned around that huge deal, his little buddy would never have gotten that extra deal. After the meeting, they each found me separately to tell me that they had stood up for me. During many times in my career, men have tried to take credit for my work, but I vividly remember two times leadership stood up for me like this. Subtle PR pays off, and once key people see how hard you work, they might even stand up for you when you're not around.

When I coach people about under-the-radar PR, I tell them to let key people know something positive that they, or someone who works for them, have done. It should be short, sweet, and consistent. "Wow, it blew me away! Natalie from the Dragon account told me the other day that my follow-up has been impeccable, and she really appreciates that." One and done.

Or you can lift somebody up; it still reflects positively on you. "John, who takes care of all of the equipment in the company, has gone through and double cleaned everything. Even though he had a lot of work on his plate, he went the extra mile and cleaned everything. No one asked him; he just did it."

I shared this story individually with three key leaders in my company. I was walking down the hall with a rep I was coaching, and we passed someone who turned around and said, "Hi, Lori!" It was a highly successful sales rep at a competitive company. She looked at the rep I was with and said, "Do you know who you're working with?" He shrugged. She had a puzzled look on her face, like, "Really, dude?" Then she blurted out, "She's a legend!" I knew she was no slacker either. I thanked her; that meant so much to me.

The key is to be genuine. That comment did, and still does, mean a lot to me. Or perhaps you start with a negative situation and show how you turned it around. Perhaps your manager hears your story and says, "I love how you handled that objection." Then, hypothetically, your manager asks you to share it at the next sales meeting. That would be a great indication that your name is solidly on the map.

When doing your own PR, there are three main keys: being consistent, using fresh material, and delivering the info in a subtle way. Being consistent doesn't mean repeating the same thing twenty times to the same person like I did. It means making sure that a few different people know the same things. Maybe you share in a group with a few key people in it or share in a few different circles.

The same story starts to look like bragging pretty quickly, so use fresh material. You're consistently doing great work, so keep the new stories coming! Don't wait and worry over finding the perfect scenario to share. Fresh material could be:

- Positive comments or gratitude from customers or colleagues
- Something great that happened on a call
- A negative situation you managed to turn around
- Accomplishing company goals or to-dos no one has gotten around to doing
- Working early, late, or on the weekend
- Making introductions
- Making the company look good
- Mentoring a new or struggling recruit
- Going over and above for an account

For example, you, the rep, get a last-minute call from a surgery center. The account is low on stock of a product they need for several upcoming cases, so they ask for one extra. You, a female knight in shining armor and stealthy salesperson, bring three extra products, just in case. In this case, my under-the-radar

PR suggestion is to leave a note for the key individual, letting her know that you handled it and perhaps adding the time in the top corner of the note. If the time is dramatic—say you dropped it off late or super early in the morning to make sure they were set for the day—even better. Now, this doesn't mean you should purposefully drop it off late or early; that's contrived and slimy. But when you're legitimately going above and beyond, there's no reason to be secretive about it.

After mentioning this idea to a male rep I was coaching, he told me he thought it was contrived. Of course, he did. All he had to do was show up breathing, and he was all set. As a female rep, it's a different story. We often have to work harder and smarter to get on the radar because the assumptions people make aren't always in our favor. Confidence leads to promotions, and men can often lean on their confidence without having the material to back it up. On the other hand, women often have far more material—product knowledge, preparation, skill sets, happy customers—without demonstrating that same confidence. Therefore, I always believed in capitalizing on every ounce of the good deeds I was doing. I had no problem in both going the extra mile and writing down the damn time.

Of course, it's your choice. I told the male rep to feel free not to do it. But my goal is for women to think differently about subtly promoting themselves, especially when we're constantly doing the right thing and over-delivering in our jobs. What's wrong with subtly making sure it gets a little notice? It's consistently delivering with a flair. If you've been putting in the extra time or helping out a new recruit, the boss may notice. On the other hand, if you've been doing it for a few weeks and no one has noticed, maybe you mention it. Teamwork is usually highly valued, and onboarding new people is often a challenge for many organizations. If you're inclined to help someone out, this is a win-win for everybody.

And finally, you'll need to practice delivering your information in a subtle way. It's important not to confuse what I'm suggesting with being a suck-up, and it's always better to underdo the PR than overdo it. Remember my example. You definitely don't want it to come across as, "Look what I did, Mom!"

Great, subtle PR could be as simple as mentioning a story that happened and how you handled it. Stories, including secondhand comments, will always come across better than sharing directly because you're showing rather than telling, and actions speak louder than words. If it feels awkward, remember that managers hear about problems all day long and appreciate hearing about things that have gone well. Additionally, when you look good, you make them look good!

Let's say that about once a week, you share a positive story, and it just so happens to make you look good. You might start the conversation like this: "When you have a minute, I've got a story for you. I think you're going to get a kick out of it!"

If you think you've been doing too much personal PR, you're probably right. Take a break. Pick back up occasionally with a story you're proud of. Also, keep an eye on the reaction. If your boss seems less than interested or acts like she would rather watch paint dry, maybe you need to reevaluate who you're telling. Under-the-radar PR is not only for your direct boss; it's for customers/clients and people in the different tiers of your organization.

Think about your PR campaign. Who are the people you need to subtly keep in the PR loop? It doesn't necessarily have to be the same person or same people over and over. All of it will add up. Just make sure you're not going to lose your proverbial single basket of eggs if someone quits. Additionally, don't waste your PR on an individual who tends toward insecurity or jealousy because it will vaporize. Instead, find a handful of people—about three—who like you and want you to do well.

These are the people who will spread your PR, not bury it. They should also be key players somewhere in the organizational structure. They will have the incentive and the opportunity to help boost your signal. If you do come across a bad leader, boss, customer, or coworker, don't let them define how you show up. Keep doing the right thing and putting those good deeds out there. Believe me, it will pay off.

Don't waste your PR on an individual who tends toward insecurity or jealousy because it will vaporize. Instead, find people who like you and want you to do well. These are the people who will spread your PR, not bury it.

It doesn't matter what level of business or career you're in. Subtle PR is essential in playing an active role in your career, in getting recognized for your talent, getting noticed for the right things, and moving up through the ranks.

Never Get Carried Away by Your Own Perfume

Shout-out to my mother, who taught me this years ago. She said to never get too full of yourself. It will hurt you in your life and your career. She was right.

I once worked with a brilliant young woman. She was crazy smart, and she knew it. She was also a smartass and made fun of anyone and everyone around her. And she wasn't someone who unified people.

When we were on a sales call together, I watched her make subtle fun of our customer in front of one of the customer's peers. As I tried to recover the bombed reference, it occurred to me the rep didn't get it.

After the sales call, I told her, "If you want to make a joke, make the joke about yourself."

Choosing to make the customer the butt of your joke is self-destruction. Even though *you* may think it's a riot, it will backfire every time. Never do it.

She was classically carried away with her own perfume. Nobody wanted to work with her. She ended up slowly imploding.

Whenever I'm talking to anyone, I lift them up. The last thing I'd say is something to make them feel bad or feel like I don't respect who they are and what they're doing.

Years ago, I was coaching another sales rep who was a complete jerk. As we walked into the account he was calling on, he looked at three gatekeepers and said, "Geez, you guys aren't busy at all!" Guess what happened. They told him to go pound sand. We had to go all the way back to the front entrance and sign in, basically starting all over again to get back to the three gatekeepers. He slammed the door shut on a total access account.

This happens within companies too. There were plenty of people (usually men) who I'd train, they'd do really well, get tapped for a promotion, and it would go right to their heads. I'd be thinking, *I remember you in sales diapers!* Classic getting carried away with your own perfume. Well, aftershave.

Stay humble. Never forget your roots. Lift people up.

If you've never gotten carried away with your own perfume, good. Keep it that way. If you can relate to this story, then steer clear and learn from it. Hit the "do not repeat" button. When you lose your humility, you instantly stop growing.

20

BUMPS IN THE ROAD

My mother taught me that where there's a will, there's a way, and that has resonated throughout my life.

In the beginning of my career in medical device sales, one of the products we often brought to accounts was a big, seventy-pound monitor. On some calls, I needed to lift the monitor up onto a stackable cart in order to bring it inside, which was a bit of a challenge. Did this prevent me from kicking ass at my job in any way? Absolutely not! It didn't take me long to realize that if I put the cart together, rolled it up snug to the curb, and locked the wheels, I could hoist the monitor out of my car, step up on the curb, and easily slide it right on top of the cart. It worked like a charm every time. Where there's a will, there's a way.

At the time, I was one of two female reps at my company. At sales meetings, the many male reps would always ask, "How do you lift the heavy monitor?" I found that question rather offensive. I could see them picturing some stereotype of a delicate female struggling with the manly equipment. Sometimes, I'd look at the guy asking me that question and say, "Is it hard for you?" That usually stopped him in his tracks, but inevitably another guy would ask the same question a few minutes later.

Sometimes, someone in my accounts would come help me, and there were many wonderful, thoughtful men who would ask, "Can I help you with that?" When I was pregnant, they may as well have just ridden up on a white horse! Yes, I did appreciate the help!

But this was an entirely different question than the male sales reps were asking. The reps' question was a lame, BS reason to try to keep women out of a medical device career—or at least keep them out of sales in that particular company. These men could not seem to grasp that there was any other way to get something done than the way they did it themselves. Obviously—well, not to the male reps—something as trivial as a heavy piece of equipment wasn't going to get in the way of me doing my job. I had plenty of ways to get that monitor where I needed it to go.

The second year on the job, I, along with three other guys, was chosen to have a film crew follow me for a day. Being chosen was a huge honor because the video would be shown at our national sales meeting attended by the entire sales division, leadership, marketing, and many staffers from around the country and the globe. An incredibly professional crew came to interview and video me.

In addition to the honor of getting to be in this video, it was also an opportunity. I wanted to shut down the BS question I always got from male reps at meetings about lifting the equipment. So, I explained to the crew what I wanted to do. I wanted them to film me successfully managing the monitor but not to show my handy shortcut using the curb. The film crew was awesome about the monitor thing, and they loved what I was trying to accomplish to reeducate the male sales force and leadership. Using a bit of ingenuity, they made it look incredibly easy for me. Creative, out-of-the-box thinking—piece of cake. They shot me putting the monitor on top of the cart, then I leaned into the camera, held both arms up, and flexed my muscles. While I don't think you could exactly see my muscles bulging, it was pretty funny. My goal was achieved. I never had another question. Plus, I don't think the new female reps that came after me were asked that question either.

Thinking outside the box is part of what women do every day to make things work. We refine angles, look at things differently, and get the damn thing done. No problem. We look at things creatively and make things happen.

I never had a single problem getting that monitor on the cart. As much as the men seemed to think that obstacle was insurmountable, it was not a problem for a woman in the medical device industry. In fact, it was an advantage; there were some smaller guys who may have also struggled with putting the heavy monitor on the cart, but I know they didn't have anybody offering to help them. It still makes me cringe when I hear something is probably difficult for women. I always want to say, "We won't be doing it the same way you do it, buddy, but we'll get it done."

We refine angles, look at things differently, and get the damn thing done. No problem. We look at things creatively and make things happen.

If I'm working and there's something difficult to deal with, I will find a way! There's no reason not to hire me because you think I can't carry something heavy or manage something difficult—I will get it done, and so will my sisters. Give us the opportunity to prove it. Do not worry about us; we are more than ready for any challenge.

Sleaze in Sales

During your professional life, you may experience a challenging situation. The following story happened after I was a seasoned saleswoman, but this kind of thing can happen to a woman at any point in her career.

There have been a few times in my career when I've had to put sleazebags in their place. Meaning a man in a powerful position tried to have sex with me. That was a mistake on their part. Thankfully, 97 percent of the doctors I worked with never did or said anything, but, unfortunately, I had to endure that 3 percent.

On one particular occasion, it was blatant and unbelievable. A doctor requested I bring in two of my products, so he could decide which one he liked better. He worked at an account of mine, and they were looking to upgrade their equipment.

I'd been selling in the medical device arena for a few years. I'd worked my ass off to build a reputation as someone my accounts knew they could always rely on. My motto was to out-service the competition daily. I had one of the highest penetrated markets in the country, meaning I'd gotten my products into almost every account in my territory.

That particular day, I was talking with the doctor and his PA (physician's assistant). The doctor asked about the price difference between the two products, and I told him it was about $10,000. His PA left to take care of something, so the doctor and I were alone.

He looked at me and said, "If you give me a blowjob, I'll pick the more expensive one."

There was no question in my mind that he was serious.

I felt my face go red hot. The palms of my hands started to sweat, and adrenaline was pumping through my veins. I'd been learning how to box, and I wanted to punch him in the throat and drop him. But my feet felt like they were in cement shoes because I knew in the back of my head this doctor had a lot of clout. He worked in several of my accounts, and he could definitely hurt my business.

I looked at that son of a bitch, and these words came out of my mouth: "Dr. Shit (only kidding, I said his name), you couldn't buy enough of my equipment to get a blowjob from me."

A couple of hours later, after the doctor had tried both products, he declared he wanted the account to purchase the less expensive one. After packing up all my equipment, I got in my car and called the big boss of my division. I told him what happened and that I was concerned for my business. I told him to prepare to talk to our corporate lawyers because I'd worked too hard in my territory to let this jackass hurt my business.

Fortunately, the doctor didn't mess with any of my other accounts. It would've been interesting to see what transpired with my company had he done so. I have no idea what the big boss did with my information because we never spoke about it again.

The biggest takeaway here is to handle the situation the best way you can. Whatever you do is the best way. You'll be able to handle it.

Nothing prepares you for that feeling. Since the amazing #MeToo movement, if someone does pull something sleazy on you, I think you'll have more support around you, and you can shine the light in their beady little eyes. Make a little note to yourself from somebody who's been around the block: you can deal with the sleazebag. It will not throw you off your goals and hard work. You'll be fine, but it's not going to go well for him.

Sometimes, You May Work for (a) Dick

I remember something that happened early on when I was working in a new industry like it was yesterday.

I'd asked for a meeting with my boss to go over questions and ideas I had regarding my territory and accounts. He told me to meet him at 7:00 a.m. at the IHOP near his house. Figuring we'd have plenty of time to cover everything, I scheduled a nine o'clock meeting with my customer.

I got to the breakfast spot a little early and had all my questions written out in my file folder. I was prepared and excited to get answers to my questions and approvals for some business items.

At 7:15 a.m., there was no sign of my boss, and I hadn't heard from him. I used the pay phone to call him. It rang and rang until he finally answered with a groggy, "Hello?" I'm no detective, but I'm sure I woke him up. I told him I was at the meeting place waiting for him. He told me he was on his way.

As it got closer to eight o'clock, I called my customer to see if I could move our meeting back a bit since I'd need at least an hour to cover the material with my manager. She was fine with that. As I was wrapping up on the phone with her, I looked to my right and saw my boss roll in nonchalantly. He came over and asked me, "Are you rescheduling your nail appointment?" One name popped into my head—dick. That was a dick thing to say. Not funny, and I have a good sense of humor.

At the end of our meeting, he told me he needed to leave town for a two-day meeting several hours away. He started to ask me something, then stopped.

When I first started working for Dick, he had me pick up something at the airport that one of the shipping companies had been holding for him for weeks. The shipping company guy was furious that they'd been holding it for so long. When he hesitated, I was mentally preparing for something like that incident.

So, I pressed him. "What were you going to ask me?"

He came back with, "Well, I hate to ask you this, but I need you to pick up my dry cleaning."

I remember thinking, *You can't be serious.* When he hesitated to ask, I assumed it was going to be something like picking up the package at the airport, which was lame but at least work-related. Instead, this was personal and ridiculous. I'm sure I had a funny look on my face. He further explained how busy he was and didn't have time to go get his dry cleaning. Biting my tongue, I asked where it was and told him I'd pick it up.

As I drove to my meeting with my customer at nine, I thought, *Is this guy for real?* It got better. Later in the day, I went to the dry cleaners. As it turned out, I happened to know the woman at the counter. She was an owner that I'd called on when I sold advertising. I explained I was there to pick up my boss's dry cleaning.

When I told her my boss's name, her face changed immediately. She looked like she had smelled sour milk—probably similar to the look on my face when my boss revealed he thought I was his laundry delivery service. The owner filled me in on my boss, who owed her over $300 for his past dry-cleaning orders. This guy had been making six figures for several years and owned a car, a house, and even a boat. It was rude and ridiculous that he wasn't paying her. Understandably, she was conflicted about giving me all these clothes since he owed her a significant amount of money. I offered to pay his bill. She wouldn't hear of it. She thought he would stiff me too. Did I mention she was a super classy woman? She cautioned me about him. I told her I'd make sure he got his ass back over there and paid.

After picking up Dick's dry cleaning, I went to his house. He, of course, was not there, so I gave his roommate all the dry cleaning. Before I left, the roommate ended up telling me that my boss never worked his territory as a rep. He was into water skiing, and the roommate told me he had been on the water the entire summer.

That would explain why he never made his quota and why many of my new customers would ask me if I was going to show up after I made a big sale. Because, as I came to find out, my boss never showed up. I had always figured the competitors weren't showing up, but I never thought my boss was the one who pulled the disappearing act. This guy just kept getting better and better.

I told his roommate that my boss owed the cleaners a lot of money and that it was going to get ugly for him if he didn't take care of what he owed in the next few days. I also told the roommate to tell him that I was the most expensive laundry delivery service he would ever have.

I never shared this story with our leadership. Instead, I held my nose and got through it. I knew the money and opportunity were going to be good in this position. Having worked for other companies where I'd seen women treated well and promoted into high leadership, I also knew that in the big picture, he was an anomaly, not the rule. I was way too new in both the company and the industry to raise a stink, and for some reason, this guy's star was shining bright. Leadership loved him. I thought he was the biggest bullshit artist on Earth. Eventually, the bullshit caught up with Dick, but it took longer and more steps up the ladder than you'd want to think.

The moral of the story is that sometimes you're going to work for Dick. Maybe it's someone piling extra office work onto you because you're a woman or someone pushing you to use sales techniques you know are wrong for you. Most of the time, you'll outlast them, so hang in there. Sometimes, you'll want to speak up. Trust your intuition and do what's right for you and your principles, goals, and reputation.

I believe it's best to keep your integrity, know who you are inside, and never let a boss or manager chip away at the good things you're trying to do. Do what's right for you because it's your career and your name on the line, not some clueless individual who's taking up temporary space in your sales career. You only have to answer to yourself!

21

ASK FOR HELP

Sales is not about figuring out the one best technique and using it in every situation from day one to eternity. Part of why sales is such an interesting and rewarding career is because everything is so versatile. You work with many personalities, industries, companies, and values, and you encounter all sorts of things. To respond to this constantly changing landscape, a successful salesperson must be versatile and adaptable. Know your stuff, but also know when to use it. It's not enough to create a great toolbelt; you also need to know how to use the best tool for each situation and how to adapt it for that unique set of circumstances. Be constantly on the lookout for new ideas and ways to improve. If something isn't working, let it go. If someone else has advice about how to get better, take it with gratitude and use it to grow!

There are all sorts of reasons you might need to ask for backup. Asking for help is a powerful move. When done correctly, it can move you forward.

Lay Down the Law

Recently, I reconnected with one of my favorite people I ever coached in sales. Let's call her Super Rep. She reminded me of a story from when we worked together in medical device sales.

Back when I was coaching her, she told me about a doctor's office where the staff had been really difficult, shutting her out from meeting with the doctor. But they had no problem eating the homemade salted caramel chocolate tarts she brought them. Maybe they thought she could expense all that and it wasn't a big deal, but it was. She was making delicious food for them, spending her own money to pay for the ingredients, and spending time making the labor-intensive dish.

She took me in to meet with the nurses and the staff to see if there was a way to get past this homemade salted caramel chocolate tart-eating group. Empty-handed, we talked with the staff. Since it's never productive to come in guns blazing, the conversation started out casual but firm.

I said, "I'm not sure you all are aware, but Super Rep pays for these ingredients and makes these labor-intensive dishes for you all on her own time. She'd like the opportunity to meet with Dr. Hidden. Dr. Hidden may appreciate the products she has to show him. I believe she's earned the opportunity to get in front of him. How do we make that happen?"

They'd been taking advantage of her. It wasn't right or fair. She was trying to earn a living and needed an opportunity to get in front of the doctor.

I felt a mixture of guilt and cluelessness emanating from the group. It was partially understandable. The staff was used to getting things from other reps who sold a completely different line of products. Those reps had an endless amount of reimbursed expenses available. But Super Rep was different. Her expenses weren't covered, and she was doing everything she could to get in front of Dr. Hidden. After our short but sweet conversation,

Super Rep booked her meeting with Dr. Hidden's scheduler. It was a success all around: Super Rep had her meeting scheduled, and that crew was about to get some reward dessert.

Sometimes, you need help from somebody else to make people understand. Choosing the right help is important. While bringing someone with more seniority helps, the most important thing is trusting that person. Do you trust that the person you're asking for help is going to help you? What's their motivation? Are they a team player? Will they benefit when you accomplish what you're trying to accomplish? Are they someone who gets it and is a mentor? Are they diplomatic? Will they be successful if you bring them in? The last thing you want is to ask someone to come with you and have them make the situation worse. You must trust that the backup you're bringing is there for you and nothing else.

Choosing the right help is important.

Once you figure out who to take with you, explain the situation and what you want to accomplish. Many times, taking your manager is all you need. But if you have a manager who lives in another part of the country, you may need to use someone else who's closer. Having someone in your company who can give a new perspective to the client/customer can help you get through the difficulty.

Sometimes, people resist asking for help. I understand. Women are extremely tough, and we know we are movers and shakers. It's hard to ask for help. Who wants anyone to know they don't know everything? But the gig is up. It's impossible to know absolutely everything. The "fake it 'til you make it" line is bullshit when you're having trouble with something. It's okay to feel like you're in over your head or need someone to help you get your bearings. If you're honest with yourself and look at why you're struggling, mention it to someone who can help. Empower yourself by strategically asking for guidance, support, direction, or whatever you know you need. Don't let insecurities stop you from becoming even better at what you do. The better you get, the more you'll understand that it's okay to ask for help, and for heaven's sake, support and help someone who asks you. Pay it forward, and we'll all be better.

And yet, there's a difference between asking for help and being helpless. Being helpless or making it seem like you can't do it for yourself is a hard stop. The damsel in distress is ridiculous and useless. Instead, come from a position of power, and say, "I understand this, but I'm having difficulty with that. I need some help, and then I can take it from there."

Getting Past the Grudge

I was working hard to convert a big account to a product that was going to be used every day. Three-quarters of the account was on board with my product; people were happy with it and wanted to use it. But one key decision-maker—let's call him Lame Guy—was a brick wall. For months, he kept coming up with BS reasons not to let the deal go through. It wasn't about the product; it was about me. Even though I took great care of the account and his specific department by providing a consistently high level of service, it didn't matter. Even though any time a piece of equipment wasn't working, I was always there that same day—without fail—but it didn't matter. To underline the fact that Lame Guy didn't like me, when he left, I sold over $200,000 of equipment to the female nurse who replaced him.

I knew I needed backup with Lame Guy. He wasn't going to agree to anything as long as it came from me, so I called in a colleague from our marketing department. He was a former NFL player who'd always had my back and who I knew would get Lame Guy's issue out and up on the table. One way or another, we were going to get to the bottom of it.

When we sat down, my backup looked pretty intimidating sitting at the small round table in a tiny room.

Big Guy: Do you like how well Lori services and takes care of all of the equipment in your department?

Lame Guy: Yes.

Big Guy: Once you finally get this product, Lori will actually get paid for all her work. Every department in this hospital wants this product. You're the only holdout. What's the problem?

It was easy to see that Lame Guy was intimidated, and his bluff was called. There was no problem. Checkmate. Lame Guy finally said, "I will approve it."

Sometimes, you need a heavyweight to help you over the hump. Once Lame Guy knew his bluff was called and he had no rational reason for shutting out me or my product, he had to move out of the way.

Pushing the Envelope

A rep I was working with in a major market told me she'd been trying to get the chief operating officer at a hospital to sit down with her to discuss a significant proposal. He kept putting her off. There was no reason to keep jerking her around. I told her to take me to his office. We asked around and found out he was in a meeting but should return within the hour. So, we camped out. When he returned to his office, the rep once again tried to set up a time to see him.

The COO said he could meet with her in a couple of days. This was on track with his typical M.O., which was to set something up and then cancel before the appointment. I knew we needed to push him.

Me: Thank you, but that's not going to work. We can meet today or first thing tomorrow morning.

COO: I get in really early. I'm here at 6:45 a.m.

Me: Works for us. We'll see you then.

The following morning, we met with the COO. Even though the information he shared was disappointing, we learned a lot more about him and what the account needed moving forward.

It would have been harder for the rep to make this push by herself. Having me there to back her up changed the dynamic with the COO. It gave us a reason to say no to a later meeting and interrupt his usual tactics.

Scapegoat

Another rep I was working with needed to introduce herself to people at an account and figure out who the key people were. When we got to the right spot, we found out the people we wanted to meet were all in a meeting. Since we didn't have an appointment with any of them, we could have had our ass handed to us and been kicked out. But the rep was getting stalled, and I believed it was now or never. We needed to camp outside the door and wait for them to walk out, introduce ourselves, and get some appointments booked. It was a risky move, but I could take the heat, and she could blame it on me if we got in trouble. It turned out to be a stealthy strategic move. We talked to everybody, set the appointments that we needed, and took off.

If you're in the weeds, ask for help. It doesn't make you weak; you're stronger for recognizing and getting what you need.

I'm not telling these stories to say you can't move the ball forward on your own. But having a heavyweight with you can sometimes help move things along. They might be more senior and experienced. They might be able to move you past some customer's particular grudge or bias. They might be able to take the heat if a risky move goes south, or they might be a new voice to back you up in a way that wouldn't work if it were just you.

If you're in the weeds, ask for help. It doesn't make you weak; you're stronger for recognizing and getting what you need.

What's Getting in Your Way of Greatness?

Pessimistic Paul was beaten down when I went to work with him. He had been on the job for a year and a few months, and he hadn't made his quota. His boss really liked him, but he wasn't exactly making it rain. He had two young children, and he and his wife were barely able to make ends meet. He had $20,000 in student loan debt. They were upside down in a house they owned in another state, which they were trying to sell for a profit while renting the house they now lived in. A family member was watching their children while they both tried to earn enough to keep food on the table, and he didn't have a quiet place to think or work on strategies and proposals.

On our first day, I saw that Paul had enormous potential. He had a great way with customers and was extremely conscientious. On the second day, as he was unloading all his equipment at the account we were visiting, he told me he was planning to quit his job. You could have knocked me over with a feather. Knowing that he had the talent but was so miserable that he thought he had to leave his job was a lot to take in.

I told him, "Table that thought. Let's get through the day, and we'll talk about everything afterward."

Later, he told me all the things that were weighing him down—the debt, the house, all of it—and it seemed like he had an albatross around his neck. In a Samuel Taylor Coleridge poem, mariners are punished for killing an albatross—which are a sign of good luck when alive but bring a curse when killed—by having to wear it around their neck. It's a burden, curse, and obstacle. This was exactly what Paul was feeling. His burdens were crushing his spirit and drive. He was defeated before he even left the house.

The way I saw it, Paul's financial burdens and all his other responsibilities were choking the life out of him and hurting his productivity exponentially.

I said, "These things are the albatross that is weighing you down. Sell that house, even if you take a loss. You need to get it off your plate, to unburden yourself."

Next, I told him to sit tight regarding his student loan debt; he was going to make enough money to pay that off. I also told him to find a place in the rental house where he could have a little desk, put up a dry erase board, and concentrate, so he could strategize and focus on his goals.

I continued, "About quitting your job—think about it: If you quit now, you'll go even further into debt. You'll be looking for another job and will go backward with your financial challenges. Trust me, I know you can do this. Stay where you are, work excruciatingly hard, and I will help you close business and make your quota. You'll get to the top of the mountain." We both got choked up.

As I laid out my recommendations for a plan to unload the albatross and allow him to move those obstacles aside, he seemed to realize he could shake off some of his burdens and change the path he thought he was on. Paul started to look hopeful. I told him he simply needed an opportunity to be the best he could be.

I promised him that I'd work with him by phone daily, weekly, or monthly, whatever he needed. We could talk through strategies and creative ideas, so he could make his quota and get on the right track financially. He took me up on my offer.

When I left Positive Paul, he seemed much lighter. He had a smile on his face and was focused on the future. He was planning to make a little office for himself in the basement of the rental house. He spoke to the realtor and unloaded his old house by significantly lowering the price. He promised to work hard and give everything he had to his job.

Positive Paul took on his territory like a champ. I showed him how to be more assertive and provided techniques to help him get more business, put together strategic package proposals, and make it through this challenging time. Soon, Positive Paul was starting to get it. He knew he could do it. He was on the other side now, and the albatross was starting to release its grip around his neck.

For the next few months, we reviewed his accounts and meeting strategies, and soon he started to come into his own and hit his rhythm. He called to tell me that he and his family toasted me on Thanksgiving from their new house. He wanted me to know that he'd surpassed his quota, paid off his student loan, and felt like Hercules. He made over $300,000 that year and made a good living for years to follow. He even ended up being promoted to a management position and had me come work with his people.

Getting started in sales, or going through a difficult time in sales, can rock your world. The lean times can be incredibly challenging. During those times, ask yourself: What is your albatross? Do you have personal or financial burdens that affect your productivity? What's stopping you from going all the way with your career? What are you willing to do to get there?

Sometimes, you need to discuss these answers with a person you trust to get an objective view about what's getting in your way. Then figure out a plan to get around those obstacles. It could mean letting go of something in the short term, so you can be fully productive for the future.

22

PERSEVERE

Perseverance isn't about handling every sales situation like a full-court press on the basketball court. If you do that, you're sure to alienate customers, left and right. Perseverance is being relentless in your quest. It's staying on top of and being focused on whatever goals you're seeking. This is vital, especially during the trickier times in your sales career. Sales has its highs and lows, and sometimes you need to put your head down, slog through the mud, do the best you can, and do what you need to do to support yourself—talk to a mentor, work with a sales veteran, visit a great customer, or pick up a kickass, inspiring sales book like this one. Do whatever you need to do in order to stay in the mix. When you persevere through the challenges and are relentless in your quest, you may surprise yourself as you achieve exactly what you want.

Days of Doubt: A Pep Talk

Maybe you picked up this book because you felt doubtful about your current career in sales. Or you may be wondering if you should even choose a sales career because you doubt your ability to sell, doubt your financial future, or feel unsure of your standing with your company or boss. I hear you. I've been there before. Doubting your choices and doubting yourself is normal. It means you're pushing yourself, and it can help you perform better by contributing to your productivity and growth. As long as you don't allow the fear of the unknown to paralyze you or get into your head too much, you'll be fine.

Right after I graduated college, I got a huge opportunity back home in Charlotte. Almost as soon as I accepted the offer, I was on the phone with my best friend, scared of the unknown. Most of my worry was focused on it being difficult to get around; I'd only driven within a ten-mile radius of my home. I was worried about my huge territory. I even doubted my abilities to do the job. This was my first professional opportunity, and I was downright scared that I couldn't pull it off.

As it turned out, as soon as I started driving everywhere, it was a moot point. I had no trouble at all. Once I got in there and started doing the job, I took to it like a fish to water. My worries vaporized as soon as I applied myself to the task at hand. Often, your biggest worries or doubts end up being no big deal. In fact, after that driving conquest, I never worried about driving anywhere again.

The brutal part of doubt is when you start believing it. That's dangerous. When you feel doubt creeping in, take a deep breath and figure out how to use the doubt to help you be more productive or to look at the big picture in a different way. Maybe you're working on an extremely important deal. You know you have to succeed, so the pressure is on. Then you start to doubt that you're going to win it. That's totally natural. Instead of wigging yourself out, figure out what else you can do to be even more prepared to get the deal. What will give you a mental advantage and make you feel even more like you have that edge? For me, sometimes, it was running everything by someone I truly respected to see if there was anything I'd overlooked or left out. Sometimes, I'd review things out loud. Sometimes, I'd talk to different people at my company or at the account, just to make sure I had all my ducks in a row. Tying up the loose ends and questions made me feel as mentally prepared as possible.

When you feel doubt creeping in, take a deep breath and figure out how to use the doubt to help you be more productive or look at the big picture in a different way.

Focus on what you can control: how you show up, smiling, maintaining a good attitude, working hard. If you have a few customers you really like to see, make sure you keep them in the rotation. Stop and think of all the big and small accomplishments you've achieved in your life. Remember the things that worked out or came together that you never expected.

I had doubts about writing this book. In fact, it was more of a fear of the unknown. Even though people have told me, "You ought to write a book," doing it and putting myself out there is risky. Would it be helpful? Would women want to read it? Would people buy it? Would they like it? Would they think I'm full of beans?

It's okay to doubt yourself, just don't let it consume you or run you. Push through it, sister! The good stuff is on the other side. Your payoff will be whatever you learn or achieve.

Sometimes, my doubtful inner critic can cause a lot of havoc and too much doubt. Over the years, I've learned to tell her to go pound sand. That's why I'm writing this book, and that's why I've done what I've done in my career: because I believe in myself, and I choose to push through it. I hope this gives you strength to stick to your resolve and not let doubt or the fear of the unknown stop you from what you're capable of doing.

I encourage you to get uncomfortable and go after what you want. If you want it badly enough, you'll have the guts to earn the glory. Give yourself a pat on the back and a little pep talk. Look at your reflection in the mirror every morning and tell yourself, "You've got this, baby!"

Playing Hardball: Advocate for Yourself

Negotiating for yourself and your income is absolutely as important as negotiating on behalf of your company—even more so. If you don't do it, who will? When playing hardball, go big, go high, hold your ground, and know your value.

Go Big, Go High

When I had my daughter, I decided I wanted to be with her and not in accounts all day, every day. My company had been sending a lot of people for me to train in my territory, so I thought I could help our sales organization by going on the road to coach new sales reps in their own territories once a month. I knew I could teach them how to effectively cold call on customers, identify opportunities, organize and close deals, and run their territories well. I could help fast-forward the learning curve for new sales reps. Plus, it would be an advantage for the sales coaching to happen in the rep's territory.

When I first started going on the road, I went for three to five days, once every seven weeks. The rest of the time, I was with my daughter, so instead of working in my territory every day and writing proposals or correspondence every night, I was home.

I was handing over the reins of my territory in September and had made my year-to-date quota for the year so far. When upper management was aware of my plan to leave the company, I told the VP of sales that I wanted to be paid my bonus. He said they didn't do that; the only way they paid bonuses was if somebody made their quota and finished out the year. I told him I could make my year-end quota by the end of September. And if I did, I wanted to be paid my bonus even though I hadn't technically finished the year as an employee.

The VP didn't agree on that phone call, so I went to run a few errands, leaving him to think about what I said. Silence is a strong technique in closing, and this was a negotiation like any other. By the time I came back to my office, he'd left a voicemail saying they were absolutely willing to pay my bonus if I made my quota, whether I made the quota for the whole year or year to date. He said they valued me that much.

Of course, I made my year-end quota by the end of September. The VP invited me to the national sales meeting and said they would give me my bonus check then. That's when I made my move. I told him I wanted to sit down with him at the meeting and run an idea by him. He agreed, so I set up a lunch date with him. I told him I could increase the effectiveness of new reps by teaching them how to strategically work their territories and increase their effectiveness in front of the customers. He liked the idea, and I started training new reps the following month.

These two different stories underscore the importance of advocating for yourself and knowing the good stuff you bring to the table. Even though both of these scenarios happened at completely separate times, it shows that knowing your value and asking for what you want will serve you well. When you bring great value and benefit an organization, you have more leverage to advocate for whatever you want.

Know Your Value

I was once called in to try to save a deal worth over $600,000 dollars; I told you about that in a previous chapter. I was a sales coach at that point, independent from the company, and the company president asked me to save the deal from the embers.

The first thing I said to him was, "Let me get this straight—you're sending me into a house on fire to see if I can bring out the coffee table? If I don't get the deal, are you going to judge my sales coaching skills on the fact that I couldn't get the deal turned around? Especially since I'm not the rep, and the last three reps have done a terrible job and hurt our company's reputation?"

"We're losing this deal," he said. "You're our only chance at saving it. I won't judge you on whether you get it or not."

I told him that he needed to pay me whether I got the deal or not. Reputation is great and all, but my time and skills are valuable. He agreed, I went in, and I did manage to turn things around. I found the coffee table and ran out the door with it. I was able to capitalize on my reputation, including taking care of customers and having great relationships with doctors.

Many times, women don't stand up for our own unique value. We bring a ton to the table. Over the years, I've watched men be promoted (remember "Dick?"), have opportunities, and make more money because they have a certain amount of bravado about them. Let me be clear: I've worked with a ton of tremendous men. I'm not talking about them here. I'm talking about the male who is full of bullshit that burps and gets promoted, who doesn't have half the talent you have, comes across as incredibly confident, and is allowed a shot at increasing his position and income.

Once you learn how to sell and you know you can do it, put yourself in a strong earnings situation. As you become a sales contender, you have the value of flexing your muscles when you need to. Negotiating or talking with a leader who understands what you're made of can help you capitalize on your value. Obviously, you'll have to prove yourself first, but once you establish yourself, you can negotiate for more.

The squeaky wheel gets the grease. With that being said, you don't want to be somebody who's always asking for money or complaining about money. I've seen men and women both do that, and it's annoying. I prefer to be someone who knows my value and will ask for what I want or walk away if they don't see the value in keeping me.

You're ~~Not~~ Going to Make It

No one, and I mean *no one*, knows what you're capable of, especially a man. There will be times when you'll run across some negative chatter. People who tell you that you don't have what it takes, it's an uphill climb, or whatever. Maybe they're mean, maybe they're jealous, or maybe they're just miserable humans. Whatever they are, their chatter is not your business. Stay on track, continue working hard, stay focused, and be professional. Use that negative comment like fuel. Think of it as wood or coal and throw it into your steam engine because you're a locomotive, baby, and you're damn sure going to crush whatever you put your mind to.

Once, when I was driving a prominent surgeon to the airport after he'd been teaching a lab, I remember being surprised at the "advice" he gave me. I was fresh out of the gate and had recently started my career in medical device sales. I was brand spanking new to that industry, although I had years of sales under my belt.

He told me—just to help me out, he said—that nurses weren't going to like me, and I was going to have a hard time with surgeons who were used to having men call on them. I asked him why the nurses weren't going to like me.

"Because you're attractive," he said.

He assumed that most nurses were women and that women don't like attractive women. He went on to say that most surgeons wouldn't be crazy about me either because they were used to working with men and weren't going to take me seriously, simply because I was a woman. They wouldn't see me as an equal. I think he thought that nurses weren't as powerful as doctors because doctors were male, and nurses were female.

I listened to everything he said, but I knew in my gut he was wrong. He was generalizing, and I was only new to medical devices, not to sales. I knew I could work hard and win people over. As one of two female reps out of nearly seventy-five in my company, I was familiar with being a customer's first female rep, and I knew way more about navigating sexism than this guy. Hello, mansplaining! I knew I could kick ass and do a great job with doctors and nurses alike, doubts and sexist assumptions be damned.

Have you ever had a conversation with someone, and they say something like, "I've got a friend who thinks blah-blah-blah?" At some point, it dawns on you that the person is talking about themselves and not a friend. That's kind of what happened with me. After dropping him off at the airport, I started thinking that this big-time surgeon from Dallas was a narrow-minded guy sharing his own ridiculous generalizations under the guise of "other surgeons" and "for my own good."

Looking back, it's funny because the nurses were a huge part of my success. I could not be more grateful for what those nurses taught me and helped me to become; I'd never have been as successful as I was without them. Of course, there were a few nasty nurses, but 95 percent were unbelievable, and I adored them. I wanted to do a great job for them. And every time I had a great connection or got a compliment from a nurse, I'd think, *Ha! Nurses won't like me, my ass.*

As for the surgeons, the Dallas doc could not have been more wrong about them either. My doctors wanted a rep who knew their product inside and out and could take care of issues immediately, somebody who didn't cut and run when things got tricky. As soon as they realized I was there in good times and bad and that I knew my products, they were great with me. I had more access and better relationships than a lot of male reps did. Once I proved myself to those doctors, I was in.

In fact, one of my busiest doctors was the surgeon for one of the sports teams in town, meaning that he had a lot of clout in purchasing decisions. He told me he wrote a letter to the leadership at one of my company's competitors, which had a ton more products than my company did, and told them they should hire me because I was a great rep. The company never reached out to me, but it meant a ton to me that one of the busiest, most respected doctors in my territory did that.

In my first professional sales position, I remember coming into our company's lobby, sweating in the hot summer humidity after working my ass off all day. I ran into one of the television station's big managers, one of those who had interviewed me. I didn't mind; I was proud he was seeing—and probably smelling—the evidence of how hard I worked, coming back in the late afternoon, sweaty after all that hustling. He asked me how it was going. I said it was going great, and I was finding a lot of new business out there. He said he had heard I was doing well. He went on to tell me all about how he and some other people thought I was never going to make it. Man! That stung a little, and it made me mad. I thought, *That's funny. Then you people weren't as smart as I thought you were.* I walked away, ready to bend a piece of steel with my bare hands. His comment put even more fire in my belly.

Years later, I now welcome that sort of attitude. I think, *Please, underestimate me! I'll enjoy breaking down any barriers you think are going to stop me. You'll see I'm not easily deterred and will not let your negative perceptions get in the way of my accomplishments.*

Years ago, people who drove many miles for work (like truckers and my dad, who was a manufacturer's rep) used to communicate on CB Radios. These radios were a great way for drivers and truckers to alert each other of accidents, directions, information, and where the state patrol was ticketing speeding vehicles. But when the radio was idle, you could hear chatter between other drivers that sounded kind of far away. That's how you should think of those negative things people may say; it's only distant chatter. You don't need to pay close attention or dignify it with a verbal response. Respond with action. Keep doing what you know is right, and don't heed the chatter. Or even better, use it to fuel you.

The Merge Philosophy

My dad drove hundreds of thousands of miles as a manufacturer's rep, and he had strong opinions about both driving and sales. He was usually proven right in the end, even if I didn't always accept it as a teenager. He knew his stuff, and even better, many of his lessons about driving also applied to life.

My dad taught me how to drive and the many subtleties of being on the road: how to drive defensively and strategically, how to communicate with truckers and give them plenty of room, how to get in the left lane when you see a car or truck pulled over on the side of the road. He said you never know when someone will open a door or walk around the vehicle, and you could accidentally hit them, so give them plenty of room.

My dad had a specific philosophy about merging: "Keep looking where you're going, have your blinker on, and for God's sake, give it gas!" He explained that too many people didn't know how to merge. He said you have to ramp up your speed, so you can closely match the momentum of the other cars already moving at a high rate of speed.

"Give it hell," he said. "Don't look back; they'll make room for you!"

When I think about the times in my career when I felt frustrated—when I found out someone didn't think I was going to succeed, thought I couldn't handle the weight of some piece of equipment, or that the nurses, doctors, or whoever weren't going to want to work with me—I used my dad's merge philosophy:

Give it hell. Don't look back; they'll make room for you! Like a lot of lessons my dad taught me, he was right.

A funny thing happens when you continually work hard, keep your head up, stay positive, and give it gas: people start to change their minds. I like making a name for myself in a positive way and changing the preconceptions people might have of me.

Hopefully, things are going swimmingly well for you, and you just bought this book for a little light reading. If not, and you're feeling frustrated, burned out, or not sure what to do, use the merge philosophy. Sometimes, a career in sales can be challenging, but you're tougher than most, so start merging!

"Give it hell! Keep your eyes on where you're going, and don't look back. They'll make room for you!"

CONCLUSION

You have many outstanding choices for a career in sales. There are multiple industries that need women like you to represent and sell for them. It's up to you to build your own empire. The themes that I've given you throughout this book are hard work, perseverance, awareness, positive attitude, and connecting with people. Women are uniquely gifted and have the potential to possess all these characteristics from the get-go.

It's up to you to build your own empire.

If you're thinking about a sales career, talk to people in sales and ask them lots of questions; do your homework. If you're in the early years of your sales career, let's talk. I can help you get off on the right foot and quickly launch into a successful, profitable, and rewarding occupation. If you're in a sales rut, I hope you can use the important tools outlined here to take your career to the next level.

Now that you have read this book and learned some of my best Stealth Sales Secrets, it's time to take the next step to increase your effectiveness in the field. Please email me at info@StealthSales.net for your free list of "The Seven Stealth Sales Get Fired Up Techniques," or visit the Contact Me page on the Stealth Sales website at www.stealthsales.net and leave a personal message. I'd love to hear how this book has impacted you. I always love connecting with my readers.

What are you waiting for? Time is money, and it's your time to earn the big bucks!

ACKNOWLEDGMENTS

Special thanks to . . .

My amazing daughter, Claire. From the very first moment I cradled you in my arms, and every day since, you've inspired me to be the absolute best version of myself. You don't know this, but you're the reason I wrote this book, and I am so proud of the strong, independent young woman you've become.

My friend Forrest. Your insight, encouragement, and support for writing this book have been immeasurable. We are fortunate to have a human being like you walking the planet.

My brilliant editor and niece, Megan. Thank you for getting the wheels of the locomotive back on track and churning through your patience, kindness, humor, and grace.

Amanda, my first editor and friend. Thank you for the times you gave me an encouraging pep talk and sent me back into the writing game.

Blair the Brander. You're an incredible individual with tremendous vision and knowledge. You've taken my business to an entirely different level. Thank you from the bottom of my heart.

My incredible mom and dad. Thank you for always believing in me and providing solid footing for taking on life's challenges. Your love and support were second to none.

My dear brother Scott. Thank you for always seeing the best in me and encouraging me throughout my life. You're tremendous.

My big brother Steve. Thank you for all of the things you've taught me.

Louise, you're one of the greatest humans I've ever known. You're an inspiration, and I'm blessed to call you my mother-in-heart.

Suzanne, you're a gem. Your incredible friendship has been a gift. Thank you for your undying support.

To Jana, my first mentor and best friend. I miss you every day.

Thank you to my family and friends: Jane, Jan, Joy, Drew, Rachel, Gaelyn, Lauren, Griffin, Ruby, Sandee, Gayle, Jamie, Julie, Rima, Greg, Kristin, Sarah, Hailey, Shanna, Haydn, Braden, Carter, Alex, Evan, Mike, Tim, MaryAnne, Elizabeth, Cathy, Kathi, Joe, Karen, Tammy, Mr. Kelly, Janet, Kimberly, Gilla, Pat, Dianne, Jacquelyn, Sara, Nancy, Agustin, and Ann.

Thanks to my past colleagues, people who I've had the privilege to coach, managers who gave me a chance, and clients/customers and neighbors who bought anything from me.

Author/writer Ellie Grossman-Cohn and author Lisa J. Schultz, thank you for being such great resources and inspirations.

A major shout-out to Nancy Erickson, The Book Professor®, and her team. You're tremendous to work with. Your editing and feedback have made this book ready for prime time! Thank you for your expertise.

ABOUT THE AUTHOR

Living in Denver for over thirty years, Lori Cornetta never tires of seeing the beautiful majesty of the Rocky Mountains. Whether she's riding her bike or walking along the trails near her home or participating in a yoga class or swimming laps, Lori thrives on movement and physical activity. With her beloved husband, Mark, she loves to laugh, listen to music, dance in the kitchen, and hang out on the back patio of their home.

Lori loves cooking and creating meals for her family. Recently, she's been experimenting with even more new, healthy recipes. When the smoke alarm doesn't alert the neighbors to her creative endeavors, she knows she's got a potential winner! That's when Mark, her ever-supportive husband, gets to try the new dish.

Lori is extremely passionate about continually learning, teaching, and coaching. One of her greatest joys is helping others achieve their personal and professional goals and making their dreams come true. That's why she created Stealth Sales, and that's why she's sharing this book with you.

WORK WITH ME

Regardless of your experience, I'm ready to help you get to the next level through individualized coaching.

As an experienced Stealth Sales coach and mentor, I have the skills to uncover your unique style and determine your specific needs for success. I'll further enhance your effectiveness by providing encouraging feedback and a personalized action plan to lift you up to your highest potential. The stealthy tools I've developed and used throughout my sales career are applied through coaching and solid, real-life examples to underscore the stealth message. Identifying what factors are getting in the way of sales greatness and increasing your effectiveness in front of the customer are paramount to my coaching. Through Stealth Sales one-on-one coaching, you'll fast-forward your learning curve and obtain new tools to use daily to crush your sales goals.

If you're a sales leader or business executive looking for someone to speak to your group or organization who understands what it takes to thrive in the challenging world of sales, you've found her. As a presenter, I know how to relate, motivate, and supercharge any group to new heights.

Contact me now at www.stealthsales.net or info@stealthsales. net, and let me help you get to that pot of gold at the end of your very own Stealth Sales Rainbow!

Made in the USA
Coppell, TX
24 July 2021